Criminal Justice Politics and Women:
The Aftermath of Legally Mandated Change

Criminal Justice Politics and Women: The Aftermath of Legally Mandated Change

Claudine SchWeber
Clarice Feinman
Editors

618604

The Haworth Press
New York • London

Criminal Justice Politics and Women: The Aftermath of Legally Mandated Change has also been published as *Women & Politics,* Volume 4, Number 3, Fall 1984.

© 1985 by The Haworth Press, Inc. All rights reserved. No part of this book may be reproduced or utilized in any form or by any means, electronic or mechanical, including photocopying, microfilm and recording, or by any information storage and retrieval system, without permission in writing from the publisher. Printed in the United States of America.

The Haworth Press, Inc., 12 West 32 Street, New York, NY 10001
EUROSPAN/Haworth, 3 Henrietta Street, WC2E 8LU England

Library of Congress Cataloging in Publication Data
Main entry under title:

Criminal justice politics and women.

"Has also been published as Women & politics, volume 4, number 3, Fall 1984"—p.
Bibliography: p.
1. Wife abuse—United States. 2. Rape—United States. 3. Prostitution—United States. 4. Correctional law—United States. 5. Sex discrimination in criminal justice administration—United States. I. SchWeber, Claudine. II. Feinman, Clarice.
KF9304.C75 1985   364'.973'088042   84-25213
ISBN 0-86656-364-4

Criminal Justice Politics and Women: The Aftermath of Legally Mandated Change

Women & Politics
Volume 4, Number 3

CONTENTS

INTRODUCTION

The Impact of Legally Mandated Change on Women Prisoners   1
    Claudine SchWeber
    Clarice Feinman

  Washington D.C.—Parole Inequity   3
  New Jersey—Sentencing Inequities   6

PART I: DOMESTIC VIOLENCE—BATTERED WOMEN   11

Restraining Orders for Battered Women: Issues of Access and Efficacy   13
    Janice Grau
    Jeffrey Fagan
    Sandra Wexler

  Restraining Order Statutory Provisions: An Overview   15
  Problems in the Implementation of Restraining Order Legislation   17
  Restraining Orders and the Prevention of Subsequent Abuse   19
  Methods and Data Sources   20
  Results   21
  Suggestions for Improving the Effectiveness of Restraining Orders   25

Domestic Violence in Criminal Court: An Examination of New Legislation in Ohio   29
    Daisy Quarm
    Martin D. Schwartz

  The Data   30
  Findings   31
  Evaluation   37

PART II: SEXUAL ASSAULT   47

Rape Law Reform: The New Cosmetic for Canadian Women   49
    Judith A. Osborne

  Introduction   49
  Canadian Women and Rape Law Reform   51
  Conclusions   62

Sexual Assault Prosecution: An Examination of Model Rape Legislation in Michigan   65
    Susan Caringella-MacDonald

  Introduction   65
  Michigan's Model Reform Law   68
  Application and Results of the 1974 Michigan Rape Law   69
  Conclusions   79

PART III: PROSTITUTION   83

The White Slave Traffic Act: Historical Impact of a Federal Crime Policy on Women   85
    Marlene D. Beckman

  Development and Expansion of the White Slave Traffic Act   86
  Enforcement of the Mann Act   89
  The Women in Alderson   91
  The Present Status of the Mann Act   98

New York State's Prostitution Statute: Case Study of the Discriminatory Application of a Gender Neutral Law   103
   Frances P. Bernat
Part I: Introduction   103
Part II: Buffalo Law Enforcement of the New York State Prostitution Statute   106
Part III: Conclusion   116

PART IV: CONTRIBUTOR'S CHOICES— ANNOTATED BIBLIOGRAPHY   121

"[We hold] that the right of privacy, grounded in the concept of personal liberty guaranteed by the Constitution, encompasses a woman's right to determine whether to terminate her pregnancy."

Roe v. Wade, 93 S.Ct.705 (1973)

"Does anybody know. . . where we can go to find light on what the practical consequences of these decisions have been?"

Felix Frankfurter

EDITOR

SARAH SLAVIN, *Assistant Professor, Political Science Department, State University College at Buffalo, Buffalo, New York*

EDITORIAL BOARD

KIRSTEN AMUNDSEN, *Professor of Political Science, California State University at Sacramento*
BARBARA R. BERGMANN, *Professor of Economics, University of Maryland at College Park*
MELISSA BUTLER, *Associate Professor of Political Science, Wabash College*
ELLEN BONEPARTH, *Associate Professor of Political Science, San Jose State University, San Jose, California*
IRENE DIAMOND, *Women's Studies Program, University of California at Los Angeles*
JEAN BETHKE ELSHTAIN, *Professor of Political Science, University of Massachusetts at Amherst*
JO FREEMAN, *Brooklyn, New York*
WALTER R. GOVE, *Professor of Sociology, Vanderbilt University*
MARTIN GRUBERG, *Professor of Political Science, University of Wisconsin at Oshkosh*
LYNNE B. IGLITZIN, *Associate Director of Undergraduate Studies; Lecturer in Political Science, University of Washington at Seattle*
JANE S. JAQUETTE, *Associate Professor of Political Science, Occidental College at Los Angeles*
M. KENT JENNINGS, *Professor, Political Science Department, University of California at Santa Barbara*
ALBERT K. KARNIG, *Associate Professor, Center for Public Affairs, Arizona State University*
RITA MAE KELLY, *Professor, Center for Public Affairs, Arizona State University*
JEANE J. KIRKPATRICK, *U.S. Ambassador to the United Nations*
J. STANLEY LEMONS, *Professor of History, Rhode Island University*
NAOMI LYNN, *Professor, Political Science Department, Kansas State University at Manhattan*
SUSAN GLUCK MEZEY, *Political Science Department, DePaul University*
BETTY A. NESVOLD, *Dean, San Diego State University*
KAREN O'CONNOR, *Associate Professor of Political Science, Emory University; member of the Georgia bar*
JEWEL L. PRESTAGE, *Professor and Chair, Political Science Department, Southern University*
VIRGINIA SAPIRO, *Associate Professor of Political Science, University of Wisconsin at Madison*
DEBRA W. STEWART, *Associate Professor of Political Science, North Carolina State University at Raleigh*
KENT TEDIN, *Associate Professor of Political Science, University of Houston*
SUSAN J. TOLCHIN, *Professor of Public Administration, The George Washington University*
SUSAN WELCH, *Professor and Chair, Political Science Department, University of Nebraska at Lincoln*

BIBLIOGRAPHY EDITOR

KATHLEEN A. STAUDT, *Assistant Professor, Political Science Department, University of Texas at El Paso*

BOOK REVIEW EDITOR

SHARON L. WOLCHIK, *Visiting Assistant Professor of International Affairs and Political Science, Institute for Sino-Soviet Studies, Department of Political Science, The George Washington University*

EDITORIAL INTERN

JUDY HARLA, *State University College at Buffalo*

DATA BASES EDITOR

ROBERT DARCY, *Associate Professor of Political Science, Oklahoma State University at Stillwater*

INTRODUCTION

The Impact of Legally Mandated Change on Women Prisoners

Claudine SchWeber
Clarice Feinman

Despite the frequent use of courts and legislatures as agents for remedying inequities, "it remains to be seen," as one mental health advocate has written, "whether the sweeping orders which have been obtained will actually result in [the intended benefits reaching the] beneficiaries. . . ."[1] This concern about the realistic impact of legally mandated change for the mentally disabled applies equally to women in the criminal justice system, the focus of this issue. After decades of seeking legal redress for discrimination in employment, income, education, parental rights, exclusion from jury duty, protection from domestic violence and sexual assault, differential enforcement of the laws, and so on, it is timely to document formally whether the legal successes were real or merely "paper victories."[2]

The cases selected for this volume examine what happened after the judge has ruled or after the legislature has spoken in four areas affecting women: corrections, battering in domestic violence situa-

---

Claudine SchWeber, Ph.D., is Associate Professor, Criminal Justice Program, State University College at Buffalo. Clarice Feinman, Ph.D., is Associate Professor, Criminal Justice Department, Trenton State College.

© 1985 by The Haworth Press, Inc. All rights reserved.

tions, sexual assault, and prostitution enforcement. These original studies describe the intent and subsequent outcome of court ordered or legislated change at the national and local level. They identify the "dynamics through which . . . policies [were] either translated into practice or subverted by various organizations, groups, or individuals."[3] Such analyses are important for several reasons. First, they add to the currently limited literature about the implementation of criminal justice policies. Second, they enable us to identify the factors which encourage or prevent the occurrence of the desired change. Third, they permit us to use that knowledge in designing realistic implementation and monitoring plans or to prepare for situations where strong barriers are present. Fourth, they aid in the development of theories which explain or predict the likelihood of compliance.

Most of the relevant literature on implementation in the criminal justice field comes from political scientists and practitioners.[4] They document the high incidence of failure and, like the studies in this volume, confirm that compliance rather than statutes or court orders is the critical factor in obtaining the intended change

> not only for litigants but also for states enacting. . . legislation. . . [because] the legal commands [of a court or legislature] are merely statements of rights; they are not self-executing[5]

Our interest in impact studies came from our own knowledge of cases of discrimination, the steps taken to challenge them, the legally mandated remedies, and the aftermath. These cases concerned the inequitable treatment of women prisoners. In the *Garnes*[6] case in Washington D.C., women were paroled later than men with similar sentences and circumstances; in the *Costello* and *Chambers*[7] cases in New Jersey, women received longer sentences than men with similar criminal experiences and convictions. In both instances, women sought relief first from the courts and then from the legislature. While an end to discriminatory treatment as sought by the plaintiffs was ordered by courts in Washington D.C. and New Jersey, the impact was significantly different. In *Garnes* the discriminatory practices returned after a year, while in New Jersey compliance was institutionalized by statute. As the following elaboration of these cases indicates, several factors influenced whether compliance with intended reforms was as intended.

WASHINGTON D.C.—PAROLE INEQUITY

In January 1972, Lana Phoebe Garnes et al., District of Columbia inmates housed at the federal correctional institution at Alderson, West Virginia, filed a lawsuit charging the District of Columbia Department of Corrections and the U.S. Attorney General with sex discrimination and a constitutional denial of equal protection.[8] The class action was on behalf of all women convicted of District of Columbia (D.C.) offenses serving time in federal prisons. The problem was that D.C. women* were serving more time than D.C. men with similar sentences and circumstances, because the women were paroled later. The problem occurred because the District of Columbia has no facilities for women offenders serving more than one year. These women were sent to one of five federal institutions for females located from 300 to 3000 miles away.[9] As a consequence, D.C. women in federal facilities were seen by the federal parole authorities (United States Parole Commission), whose release guidelines were more rigid than those of the D.C. Parole Board. In contrast, most D.C. male offenders were sent to a D.C. facility in nearby Lorton, Virginia.[10] They appeared before the D.C. Parole Board and were released earlier than D.C. women with similar sentences. This unusual situation, whereby federal parole authorities have jurisdiction over D.C. and federal prisoners in federal institutions, while the District of Columbia has jurisdiction only over prisoners housed in its own facilities, dates from 1934 and the protectorate relationship between the district and the federal government.[11] *Garnes* asked that the transfer of D.C. women to federal facilities be halted and declared unconstitutional. Three years later, in August 1975, a settlement was reached whereby D.C. women would remain in federal prisons but return to the jurisdiction of the D.C. Department of Corrections at least "nine months prior to their parole eligibility date. . . ."[12] This was done to permit the D.C. women from federal institutions to be heard by their own parole board, like the D.C. men at Lorton. The agreement, known as the *Garnes* Decree, together with procedures for implementation, became effective on December 10, 1976, by order of Judge William Bryant.[13]

Garnes provided that specified D.C. women in the federal system

---

*D.C. women refers only to women convicted of D.C. Code violations. The number of these women ranges from c.125 in 1980 to c.135 in 1984.

could apply for transfer to the D.C. Department of Corrections. These women had to be within nine months of parole eligibility, expiration, or mandatory release,* and had to personally request the transfer. The federal prison authorities agreed to process each request, and to send it, plus information on the inmate, to the D.C. Department of Corrections. The Department agreed to accept or reject the transfer application within 30 days and to so notify the inmate.[14] The point of this procedure was to return the woman to the custody of the D.C. Department of Corrections as quickly as possible, thereby placing her under the jurisdiction of the D.C. Parole Board.

The agreements made in *Garnes* were not carried out, although this was not discovered until 1981[15] and not corrected until 1982.[16] The federal authorities complied with their part, the processing of transfer requests nine months before the appropriate date. But, the D.C. Department of Corrections (DCDC) did not. Instead, by 1978, a year after *Garnes* took effect, DCDC only accepted transfer applications from D.C. women who had first met with the federal parole authorities and had received from them a presumptive parole date (PPD). The PPD, part of a newly instituted reform begun in 1978 for all federal prisoners, was unrelated to D.C. offenders' situation. Its intent, to give federal inmates early notice of their probable release date via parole, meant that inmates were seen and given a PPD shortly after arrival at the institution. Unfortunately for the D.C. women, the federal PPD was later than their District of Columbia eligibility date. D.C. corrections authorities, in violation of *Garnes*, were requiring that D.C. women see the federal parole board and were using the federal PPD to calculate a D.C. inmate's transfer request date.[17]** The effect was twofold: first, DCDC was

---

Parole eligibility date: the earliest date a person can be released to community supervision, as determined by statute or the sentencing judge. (In the District of Columbia, the parole eligibility date is usually set at one-third of the sentence.)

Expiration date: the final, last date of the maximum sentence, with no days off for "good time" (days off the maximum that a prisoner earns for satisfactory behavior).

Mandatory release date: the date the prisoner is released to community supervision as a result of good time or other statutory sentence reduction measures.

**For example: a District of Columbia offender in federal prison with a 6 year sentence has been given a 2 year parole eligibility date by the D.C. sentencing judge (after she has served one/third). Under the *Garnes* Decree her transfer request *should be* sent to the D.C. Department of Corrections 9 months prior to the 2 year (24 months) minimum eligibility date set at sentencing: at *15 months*. However, after arriving at the federal prison she sees the U.S. Parole Commission. Using federal standards, she receives a presumptive parole date of 2 years and 10 months (34 months). The earliest date the D.C. Department of Corrections

allowing federal authorities, rather than the D.C. Parole Board, to make decisions about the D.C. women's parole viability; second, the D.C. women's incarceration period was lengthened. *Garnes* had been signed to halt both of these practices.

The hard reality that the *Garnes* Decree was a "paper victory" was discovered and exposed by the Women Offenders Network, an organization of people in the Washington, D.C. area involved or interested in corrections, sponsored by the Women's Bureau of the U.S. Department of Labor. In 1981 the network established a task force to investigate the parole situation which inmates and persons close to the situation complained about. Task force members talked with representatives from every agency and interest group involved with the case, and asked Dr. Lucy Steinitz of the Center for the Study of Welfare Policy to research what happened to the transfer applications of D.C. women in federal facilities. The results, detailing the non-compliance with *Garnes*, were presented at the June 1981 network meeting and in Steinitz' report.[18]

The network's hard work resulted in three developments intended to bring the 125 District of Columbia women in federal prison equity with their male counterparts as regards parole. 1) A new agreement, this time between the two correctional organizations, the Federal Prison System and the D.C. Department of Corrections was signed July 1, 1982. It was designed more precisely to carry out what *Garnes* had ordered.[19] 2) Congressional hearings in 1982 and 1983, held by the Committee on the District of Columbia of the House of Representatives, aimed at examining why, in practice, the *Garnes* Decree was not implemented as ordered.[20] 3) A bill, HR 3369, passed by the House of Representatives in July 1983, to accomplish more directly, through legislative change, what the *Garnes* court-ordered change could not: give the D.C. Parole Board original jurisdiction to hear the cases of District of Columbia offenders regardless of where they were housed.[21] Until HR 3369 becomes law, which is not likely in the 1984 Congress, the parole status of District of Columbia women in federal prisons will be governed by the new agreement. Given the history of this case, continual and close

---

would accept her transfer request was at *25 months* (9 months from the 34 month federal date). As a consequence, this inmate spent at least 10 months longer in prison than she should have. Statement of Lucy Steinitz before the Subcommittee on Judiciary and Education of the Committee on the District of Columbia, House of Representatives, 97th Congress, 2d Session, *District of Columbia Female Offenders in the Federal Prison System* (May 6, 1962), p. 8.

monitoring by advocates for the D.C. women will be necessary to assure that a third agreement is not necessary.

NEW JERSEY—SENTENCING INEQUITIES

Unlike the *Garnes* case, the *Costello*[22] and *Chambers*[23] cases produced the intended reform, a gender neutral sentencing code, that went into effect in September 1979. Prior to 1979, New Jersey's sentencing codes singled out women for disparate treatment, often resulting in longer sentences for women than for men even if both had committed similar crimes under similar circumstances. Sentencing statutes for females over 16 years required that, except for manslaughter or murder, they were to receive an indeterminate to 5 year sentence (0-5 years). When the statutory maximum for that offense was less than five years (e.g., 0-3), women had to receive the maximum sentence required by law (e.g., 3 years). If the offense carried a maximum sentence longer than 5 years (e.g., 10 years), the judge could increase the indeterminate statutory maximum (e.g., 0-10 years). In all instances, incarcerated women were not eligible for work credits or for continuous orderly deportment credits. Women were also not eligible for parole by the State Board of Parole as were similarly situated incarcerated men. Rather, decisions to parole women rested with the institution's Board of Managers.[24]

In contrast, male sentences were affected by their ages and by greater judicial flexibility. Men 16 to 30 years old could receive either a reformatory indeterminate sentence (e.g., 0-5 years) or a prison minimum-maximum sentence (e.g., 10-20 years). In either case, the judge had the authority to set the maximum for that crime. Men over 30 years old received a prison sentence, but the judge could set the inmate's maximum time at less than the statutory limit.[25] This sentencing disparity which produced longer sentences for women came from the belief that:

> female criminals were basically different from male criminals, that they were more amenable and responsive to rehabilitation and reform—which might, however, require a longer period of confinement in a different type of institution—and that the legislature could validly differentiate between sexes with respect to the length of incarceration and the method of the determination thereof.[26]

In *State* v. *Costello* (1971), the New Jersey Supreme Court reviewed the state's differing sentencing statutes. Mary Costello, who was 39 and convicted of bookmaking and operating a gambling resort, had received an indeterminate to five year sentence. Her term was to be served at the New Jersey State Correctional Institution at Clinton. Since she had an indeterminate sentence, her precise release date was to be determined by the Board of Managers of the institution. Release dates were traditionally granted after the Board believed the inmate had been rehabilitated. Costello had no right to time off for good behavior or work credits. A man convicted of a similar crime under similar conditions would have received a prison sentence of one-to-two years (minimum-maximum), with his release date determined by the Board of Parole. With good behavior and work credits, he could have been eligible for parole in 4 months and 28 days.[27] In contrast, Costello could have been obliged to remain at Clinton for five years if the Board of Managers felt that the full time was needed for her reformation. Thus the New Jersey statutes mandated that women could receive longer sentences than men for similar crimes. The *Costello* court wrote that, "these distinctions, in essence, form the basis of defendant's claim of denial of equal protection because of discrimination on the basis of sex."[28] The differential sentencing issue was, however, not resolved by the *Costello* case because Mary Costello was released early from Clinton.

Another opportunity presented itself two years later. In *State* v. *Chambers* (1973), a class action suit, the New Jersey Supreme Court once again rejected the notion that females were more amenable than men to rehabilitation and therefore required a longer period of incarceration. The *Chambers* Court declared that statutory provisions for sentencing female offenders to an indeterminate sentence when a similarly situated male would receive a minimum-maximum term violated the equal protection clause of the fourteenth amendment to the U.S. Constitution.[29] In the aftermath of this decision, discriminatory sentencing practices against women offenders ended. All New Jersey women inmates had their sentences reviewed using the same criteria as that for men. Many women were released from prison.[30] This court-mandated change became part of the new criminal code effective September 1979.[31]

The favorable court decision and the effective enactment of a gender neutral sentencing code occurred during a period conducive to major criminal code reforms in New Jersey. The Governor and legislators, responding to civil rights and feminists groups, had created task forces to study sentencing disparity and sex based discrimination in the criminal codes. When *Costello* and *Chambers* filed their law suits, the enforcers of legally mandated change were already supporting the intent of the changes.

* * *

Like other studies in this volume, the Washington D.C. and the New Jersey cases show that gender can make a difference: the difficulties encountered by women in all these cases were the product of their femaleness rather than a function of their circumstances. Moreover, the point made by practitioners, that legally mandated change is just a paper victory without effective implementation, is confirmed here. In each instance the remedy was one that the women, or their allies, had sought. However, the effectiveness of the remedy—whether the desired change actually occurred—often depended on enforcement by non-allies or opponents. The impact was to nullify the original court order or statute and to necessitate another intervention by proponents, as revealed in Bernat's and Beckman's studies of federal and state prostitution enforcement. Conversely, as Caringella-Macdonald's study of Michigan's new rape law shows, support by those in charge of implementation, such as prosecutors, can have a positive impact on the outcome of legally mandated change. This pattern conforms to that noted by other researchers who argue that successful implementation is closely linked to "the disposition of people who work in the implementing agency to support the policy."[32]

An important exception to the role of this implementor variable is presented by Grau, Fagan and Wexler's nationwide examination of protective orders for battered women. They show that the ineffectiveness of the outcome may not be due to lack of enforcement, but to the inappropriateness of the original remedy (such as protective orders) to the circumstances (a batterer with a history of violent behavior).

What these case studies show, then, is that the condition of women's lives will not be changed merely by going to court or getting a new law. In part this is because "legal commands. . . are not self-executing and, without adequate provision for monitoring and insuring compliance, they will never be fully executed."[33] In part this is due to the fact that enforcement is delegated to a group less attached to the issue (perhaps even neutral or hostile) than the proponents. Thus, when the implementors of legally mandated change are opposed, or when the legal solution only imperfectly fits the problem, other acts are necessary to assure compliance. These may include infiltrating the implementation process, returning to court, establishing a significant political power base, providing social service assistance for victims and their families, creating an ongoing investigative and educational program. The political reality of equality for women is that court orders and statutes are often just the beginning of the struggle.

ENDNOTES

1. Michael S. Lottman, "Paper Victories and Hard Realities," personal Xerox copy, p. 93 (National Mental Health Association, n.d., c.1976-1980, pp. 93-105).
2. *Ibid.*
3. Merry Morash, "Introduction: Understanding Criminal Justice Policy Implementation," in *Implementing Criminal Justice Policies*, ed. Merry Morash (Beverly Hills, California: Sage, 1982), p. 7.
4. Merry Morash, *ibid.*, pp. 7-23. Morash presented a valuable brief summary and critical review of the relevant political science and criminal justice literature. See also Michael Lottman, "Paper Victories," pp. 93-105; Theodore L. Becker, ed., *The Impact of Supreme Court Decisions: Empirical Studies* (New York: Oxford University Press, 1969).
5. Michael Lottman, "Paper Victories," p. 93.
6. *Lana Phoebe Garnes, et al. v. Patricia Taylor, et al.* Civil Action #159-72., United States District Court for the District of Columbia (January 25, 1972). *Garnes* concerned other issues besides the constitutionality of transferring District of Columbia female offenders to federal facilities far from the District. These other issues concerned conditions at the District of Columbia Women's Detention Center. Memorandum and Order of Judge William Bryant (December 30, 1976) and Stipulation signed by plaintiff's counsel (January 17, 1980) and defendant's attorney (February 4, 1980).
7. *State* v. *Costello*, 59 N.J. 344 (1971); *State* v. *Chambers*, 63 N.J. 288 (1963).
8. *Garnes* v. *Taylor* at note 6.
9. The federal institutions with women, and their District of Columbia population as of May 1984:
Alderson, West Virginia (the closest to Washington, D.C.)—101
Lexington, Kentucky—18
Pleasanton, California—01
Fort Worth, Texas—01
Morgantown, West Virginia (a youth offender facility)—14
Total District of Columbia women in the federal system—135
(Total D.C. men in the federal system—1488)
10. Lorton, Virginia, is about 17 miles from the District, and holds approximately 3300 male adult and youth offenders. Carolyn Crowley, "D.C.'s Forgotten Women Prisoners," in (Washington, D.C.) *City Paper* 3:31 (August 12-18, 1983), p. 1.
11. Act of June 5, 1934, ch. 391, 48 Stat. 880 (codified in D.C. Code Ann. 24-209 (1981). This situation applies only to the District of Columbia. Inmates from states housed in federal facilities are seen by their state parole board.
12. *Garnes* v. *Taylor*, Civil Action #159-72, Stipulation of Counsel for Plaintiffs and Defendant Attorney General Concerning Designation and Return (August 11, 1975), item #8.

13. *Garnes* v. *Taylor* at note, Order of Judge William Bryant (December 10, 1976).
14. *Garnes* v. *Taylór*, Stipulation of August 11, 1975, items #2-6, 8-10.
15. Lucy Y. Steinitz, "The Garnes Decree in Reality: Parole Eligibility and Determination for District of Columbia Women in Federal Correctional Institutions" (Washington D.C.: The Center for the Study of Welfare Policy of the University of Chicago, June 1981), unpublished.
16. *Joint Agreement Between the Bureau of Prisons and the District of Columbia Department of Corrections Regarding Female Offenders*, June 28, 1982, in Federal Prison System Operations Memorandum #240-82 (5100) September 7, 1982.
17. Lucy Steinitz, "*The Garnes Decree*," p. 5-9.
18. Ilene Bergsmann, former coordinator, Women Offender Network, Washington, D.C.
19. *Joint Agreement*. . ., Karen Amy, of the Federal Prison System, is monitoring compliance with the 1982 agreement. According to Amy, the agreement is presently working as intended. Conversation of March 1984.
20. "Hearings on the District of Columbia Female Offenders in the Federal Prison System," Subcommittee on Judiciary and Education of the Committee on the District of Columbia, U.S. House of Representatives, 97th Congress, 2d Session (May 6, 1982), Serial No. 97-9; Hearings on HR 2319 (later changed to 3369) before the Committee on the District of Columbia, Subcommittee on Judiciary and Education, U.S. House of Representatives (May 3, 1983).
21. HR 3369 "A Bill to give to the Board of Parole for the District of Columbia exclusive power and authority to release on parole, to terminate the parole of, and to modify the terms and conditions of the parole of, prisoners convicted of violating any law of the District of Columbia, or any law of the United States applicable exclusively to the District. (June 21, 1983)" Passed the House of Representatives July 1983. This bill was sent to the Senate in July 1983, but no action had been taken by June 1984. If the bill does not pass by the end of the 1983-84 term, the parole bill would have to begin its congressional journey anew in 1985. Senate Committee on Governmental Affairs, Sub-Committee on Governmental Efficiency and the District of Columbia, June 1984. (Note that such a law would also apply to the District of Columbia male offenders in federal prisons.)
22. *State* v. *Costello*, 59 N.J. 334-147 (1971).
23. *State* v. *Chambers*, 63 N.J. 287-300 (1973).
24. N.J.S.A. 30:4-155; *State* v. *Costello*, 59 N.J. 342-343 (1971).
25. N.J.S.A. 30:4-148; *State* v. *Costello*, 59 N.J. 342-343 (1971).
26. *State* v. *Costello*, 59 N.J. 344 (1971).
27. *Ibid.*, 343.
28. *Ibid.*
29. *State* v. *Chambers*, 63 N.J. 288-189 (1973).
30. New Jersey Department of Corrections, conversations with staff.
31. N.J.S.A. 2C:43-1 to 2C:43-22.
32. Merry Morash, "Introduction," p. 14, citing and analyzing the works of M. Musheno, *et. al.*, C.E. Van Horn and D.S. Van Meter, and P. Sabatier and D. Mazmanian.
33. Michael Lottman, "Paper Victories," pp. 93-94.

PART I:
DOMESTIC VIOLENCE—
BATTERED WOMEN

The recent creation of a Presidential task force on domestic violence indicates that this situation has reached national crisis proportions. Contributors to this section examine the impact of two solutions commonly offered to deal with battered women: legislation that defines domestic violence as a criminal offense and courts which issue civil restraining orders.

Janice Grau, Jeffrey Fagan and Sandra Wexler evaluate how well the judicial solution—the issuance of civil restraining orders—worked in a representative national sample in 1980. Grau et al. conclude that civil restraining orders are ineffective in cases where the assailants have a history of violence.

Daisy Quarm and Martin Schwartz then examine the effectiveness of domestic violence legislation in Hamilton County, Ohio, in 1980. They conclude that making domestic violence a crime does not result in any significant change in the punishment of batterers.

The contributors demonstrate the weaknesses limiting the effectiveness of legislative and court ordered changes, and offer recommendations to strengthen the viability of both approaches.

Restraining Orders for Battered Women: Issues of Access and Efficacy

Janice Grau
Jeffrey Fagan
Sandra Wexler

ABSTRACT. Since the passage of the Pennsylvania Protection from Abuse Act in 1976, many states have enacted legislation to provide civil restraining orders for battered women. These orders, which offer a civil court alternative to criminal sanctions, are court-issued temporary or permanent orders which direct an assailant to refrain from further abusive conduct. Interviews with recipients of restraining orders suggest that the orders are generally ineffective in reducing the rate of abuse or violence. However, they were effective in reducing abuse for women with less serious histories of family violence or where the assailant was less violent in general. They were ineffective in stopping physical violence. Measures to improve restraining order mechanisms should: more clearly codify abuse and violence, improve access for those not married or cohabitating, streamline procedures and shorten waiting periods, address a full range of child-related concerns, strengthen sanctions, and mandate official responses to violations. Additionally, comprehensive legislation is needed to coordinate civil and criminal remedies.

Since the early 1970s, the phenomenon of battered women has emerged from the privacy of the family home onto the national agenda as a social problem deserving public attention. Its "discovery" was due, in large part, to the work of feminist organizations, nationally and locally, and to feminist writers and scholars

---

Research cited in this article was supported by Grants 78-MU-AX-0049 and 80-JN-AX-0004 from the National Institute for Juvenile Justice and Delinquency Prevention. U.S. Department of Justice. The opinions are those of the authors and do not reflect the views or policies of the Department of Justice.

© 1985 by The Haworth Press, Inc. All rights reserved.

who documented and publicized the issue. Having been the first publicly to define this phenomenon, grassroots women's groups across the country rapidly became aware of the array of services that victims needed: shelter, transportation, counseling, legal assistance, advocacy, jobs and child care.[1] Through their activities with and on behalf of victims they also became cognizant of the limits on available legal resources: inadequate police response, discouragement in efforts to prosecute, and civil and criminal legislation that did not provide sufficient protection for the victim.

The significance of battering as a social problem was underscored by several studies which documented that each year, approximately 1.8 million women are beaten by their husbands (or male partners in unmarried couples). The limited data available on prevalence in the general population indicated that battering occurred in at least one-fifth of all U.S. couples.[2] In the 1970s, several congressional hearings addressed the need for services and intervention strategies to ameliorate the problem. This interest at the federal level reflected growing constituent demand on municipal and state levels for increased options and more effective services for battered women.[3]

A response adopted by many states was the enactment of civil restraining order legislation to provide a civil remedy for battered women.[4] Only two jurisdictions had civil restraining order legislation prior to 1976. After 1976, passage of the Pennsylvania Protection from Abuse Act provided the stimulus for the enactment of similar legislation in 31 states.[5] Prior to these legislative enactments, the primary barrier to court access was the requirement that divorce or dissolution of marriage proceedings be initiated before a restraining order could be issued. Current legislation does not coordinate restraining order proceedings with divorce proceedings.[6]

Restraining orders are not the exclusive legel remedy available to battered women. In most states, a women who has been beaten can choose among various civil and criminal remedies. She may seek help from police, file a criminal complaint, or terminate the relationship by divorce or by other means. These potential remedies are themselves not free from problems. For example, there may be no marital relationship to terminate. Or, when assistance is requested, police response may not be adequate.[7] Women, moreover, are often reluctant to file criminal complaints against their partners. The potential relief afforded by civil restraining orders provides an attractive option for many women. However, civil restraining order legislation, criminal restraining order legislation, and criminal spousal abuse statutes are relatively recent developments and therefore somewhat experimental. A measure of such legislation's effectiveness is the degree to which it achieves its goals. One goal of civil restraining order legislation is to provide a remedy for battered women in addition to prosecution. Another goal is the reduction of violence.

This paper provides an examination of the efficacy of civil restraining orders in reducing violence against women. In the first section, a brief overview of the provisions of current restraining order legislation is presented. The second section considers problems in implementing these legislative mandates. The third section presents an analysis of data from follow-up interviews conducted in 1980 with clients four months after receiving services from federally-supported domestic violence projects. These interviews, undertaken as part of the National Evaluation of the Law Enforcement Assistance Administration's Family Violence Demonstration Program, provide victim self-reports regarding experiences with obtaining restraining orders as well as their efficacy in preventing further abuse. We found that restraining orders are most helpful when there is no history of violent abuse and when the assailant exhibits less general violence. The final section offers recommendations for improving the effectiveness of restraining orders.

RESTRAINING ORDER STATUTORY PROVISIONS: AN OVERVIEW

While restraining order statutes almost uniformly deal with court access, they do not always outline procedural requirements. Some statutes set forth most of the applicable procedures, while other statutes are more vague, presumably leaving procedures to the discretion of the appropriate courts.[8]

States may place restraining order proceedings within the civil, criminal or concurrent jurisdiction of their courts. Most states have chosen the civil court system. Venue (i.e., the location of the event which determines the appropriate court), as defined in the statutes, is either the county of residence, any county, the county where the abuse occurred, or the county of former residence, in addition to the county of residence, if the plaintiff has left the residence in order to avoid abuse.

Statutes generally require the filing of a petition to initiate proceedings. In most states it is the responsibility of the victim to initiate this process, but some states give this power to certain agencies. Frequently the petition must allege physical abuse. Although statutes rarely address the issue of whether a lawyer is needed to file the petition, in most states a lawyer is not required. Some statutes authorize the assistance of clerks for plaintiffs who do not have a lawyer and who need help preparing the petition and filing *in forma pauperis*. In addition, the statutes of most jurisdictions do not address the issue of payment of the filing fee. However, certain states waive the fee entirely or waive it upon a showing of indigency.

The lengthiness of filing procedures assumes that delayed relief, in the form of court-issued restraining orders, will not impose a hardship. Yet a battered woman often needs immediate protection from her assailant. For immediate relief it must be possible to obtain an order either without a hearing or at an immediate hearing. Prior notification of the defendant is usually not feasible under these circumstances. Most states, therefore, authorize temporary restraining orders and, in all but one, the order may be issued *ex parte*.[9]

Permanent restraining orders are most often issued only after a hearing on the petition. The order is called "permanent," even though it is of limited duration, usually for a fixed period up to one year. Types of relief available to a battered woman through the permanent order include a restraint of the defendant from further abuse, divorce-related relief (e.g., custody of minor children and payment of child or spousal support), and quasi-criminal relief.[10]

Similar to the permanent restraining order is the "vacate" order, which excludes the defendant from the residence, grants possession of the residence to the plaintiff, or orders the defendant to provide suitable alternative housing. This order affords further protection for the victim of abuse and may be necessary to ensure effectiveness of the restraining order. The court also can order the defendant to stay away from the plaintiff, the plaintiff's residence or the plaintiff's place of business. These are generally called "no contact" orders.

Once a woman has obtained a restraining order and the assailant has received a copy, the order's effectiveness in preventing abuse may be largely dependent upon statutorily mandated sanctions for violations and on police response to violations.[11] In a few states, recent statutory enactments have authorized statewide directives to law enforcement agencies regarding appropriate police response. In Massachusetts, for example, the officer is directed to use all reasonable means to prevent further abuse, including remaining on the scene if there is a danger to the victim's safety, assisting the victim to obtain medical treatment, and giving the victim immediate and adequate notice of rights. The officer is also directed to arrest the assailant when the officer has probable cause to believe a felony has been committed, or when a misdemeanor has been committed in the officer's presence, or when a misdemeanor has been committed in violation of a restraining order.

While statutorily mandated law enforcement procedures include some sanctions for violation of restraining orders, restraining order statutes themselves provide sanctions for a direct violation of an order (i.e., abusing that plaintiff when the order directs the defendant to refrain from such conduct).[12] These sanctions include civil and indirect criminal contempt, arrest and misdemeanor charges.

PROBLEMS IN THE IMPLEMENTATION OF RESTRAINING ORDER LEGISLATION

The widespread enactment of restraining order provisions would seem to indicate that the remedy is effective. However, the effectiveness of restraining orders is often limited by the very statutes which authorize them. The statutory definition of abuse, for example, omits psychological abuse, even though psychological and physical abuse may exist concurrently. In Pennsylvania, for example, the legislature explicitly rejected protection for the mental well-being of the victim. Moreover, the statutory definition of abuse rarely includes forced sexual relations (i.e., rape). Since restraining orders are designed to prevent physical violence, the exclusion of rape, which is an act of physical violence, seems to contradict the intent of the statutes.[13]

Statutorily required relationships between the plaintiff and the defendant similarly may limit court access. Depending upon the jurisdiction, restraining order legislation may apply to spouses, former spouses or cohabitators. The state may require the parties to be adults, members of the opposite sex, or involved in a close relationship. The parties also may have to live together or to have done so previously. Such statutorily required relationships serve to exclude large segments of the population from access to this remedy. The marriage requirement, for example, has no correlation with the type of person who will seek assistance, since spouses are not the only victims of battering. The exclusion of former spouses is similarly arbitrary, since incidents of violence occur among former spouses. Another common limitation is the restriction of restraining orders to persons of the opposite sex. Although physical abuse in heterosexual relationships has been studied, violence in homosexual relationships has not. Finally, the household requirement ignores the reality that some couples have longstanding relationships and/or children but have never lived together.[14]

Required procedures may also limit access. The filing fee and lack of special assistance for the indigent plaintiff who must represent herself are real barriers to obtaining a restraining order. Allowing a woman to file *in forma pauperis* as an alternative to paying a filing fee is not an adequate solution because of the delay. The indigent plaintiff, not able to afford an attorney, may be without the services of an agency or advocate who could assist her with filing procedures. The paperwork that must be completed in addition to the petition can be burdensome. Battered women who are unfamiliar with legal proceedings may not understand the legal terminology employed (for example, "plaintiff"), may not know which blanks to check on provided forms, and may not know how to obtain the judge's signature on a temporary order.[15]

While certain procedures may not impose barriers to court access, they may affect the efficacy of the relief offered. The timing of orders is critical. Studies of abusive relationships hypothesize a "cycle of violence."[16] To prevent further beatings which are part of the cycle, immediate help may be necessary. Emergency orders and *ex parte* temporary orders could provide this help, but in most jurisdictions the former is not available.[17] If the desired result is to obtain protection for the victim, relief should be immediately available, whether the remedy sought is civil or criminal. Since the type of police response sometimes depends on the existence of a restraining order, it is essential that an immediate remedy be available.

Implementation of access and enforcement procedures may not occur even when specified by statute. In some situations class action suits have been filed to gain and enforce the relief intended by the civil restraining order legislation. For example, the New York City Probation Department was charged with negligence and violations of the victims' civil rights by failing to grant temporary restraining orders. The suit also charged the police with failure to respond to violations of restraining orders and an implicit policy of avoiding arrest.[18] This failure to arrest assailants is viewed by women's rights groups as encouraging further abuse.[19] Settlement of this and similar suits included new policies for arrests for violations of restraining orders, probable cause arrests for alleged criminal conduct, and victim assistance.

The choice of sanction may also influence the effectiveness of the relief granted. Civil contempt is currently the most widely used remedy for violations of restraining orders. The victim, who is required to file more pleadings to obtain a contempt citation, may be faced with additional frustration and delayed legal proceedings. The civil contempt sanction also ignores the possibility of criminal prosecution for violation of restraining orders. Because penalties for civil contempt lie within the judge's discretion, civil contempt does not necessarily result in punitive action. Often, the outcome is a fine or a mere direction from the court to the offender not to repeat the offense.[20] If the goal is to prevent physical violence, direct enforcement, in the form of arrest or criminal sanction, may be preferable to a civil contempt citation.

To take advantage of existing legislation, the battered woman must know where to turn for help. As the topic has become more widely discussed, many victims are now aware of available help. Yet, for those victims who do not know how to obtain restraining orders and who initially contact an agency within the criminal justice system, referrals are necessary. The willingness of the police and district attorney's offices to make referrals is dependent on inter-agency cooperation or legislative mandate.[21]

RESTRAINING ORDERS AND THE PREVENTION OF SUBSEQUENT ABUSE

A primary goal of restraining order legislation is the prevention of further abuse. This section explores the efficacy of restraining orders in achieving this goal. Thus, one may ask: who obtains restraining orders? How effective are they in deterring violence? And, are there certain conditions which influence their effectiveness? While the analysis presented below is not the final word on the effectiveness of restraining orders, certain findings are significant: First, women who obtain restraining orders believe that the orders are effective in reducing abuse. Second, restraining orders are effective in curtailing verbal abuse, harassment and physical violence only when prior injuries were not severe. Third, restraining orders have less effect on reducing abuse by more violent spouses (i.e., assailants who are violent toward strangers as well as spouses or partners).

METHODS AND DATA SOURCES

Data for this study were obtained from 270 face-to-face interviews conducted with former clients of federally funded Family Violence Demonstration programs. The interviews were conducted in two panels, in the spring and fall of 1980. The clients were battered women who had sought assistance from one of the projects, and had consented to interview by an independent research team conducting a national evaluation of the federal program. Clients were interviewed approximately four months after their most recent contact with the projects. The four-month interval was chosen in an effort to balance three concerns: the problems of recall in a retrospective study; the need for a sufficient follow-up period to determine the effects of restraining orders; and the mobile and often anonymous lifestyles of family violence victims.

The family violence programs were located in four states: Florida, Vermont, Ohio and North Carolina. Accordingly, the statutory provisions varied in such respects as access, duration, remedy, enforcement and specificity. The variations were sufficiently minor so as to not effect the outcomes. All states required a civil court proceeding, although Ohio also permitted access via criminal court. The orders were in effect for 90 days to one year. Remedies included ex parte orders for 90 days and permanent orders for one year. Enforcement was via contempt proceedings in civil court, and punishment included both fines and/or incarceration for up to six months. The orders minimally stipulated no violence; some included threats and verbal abuse as prohibited behaviors. The federal mandate required that all projects focus on the justice system; the restraining order provisions were considered an important component of the deterrent underpinnings of the national program.

The research design compared the incidence of post-project incidents in the presence or absence of a restraining order. Two outcome measures of post-project incidents are used. Post-project *abuse* refers to harassment and verbal threats, as well as to acts of physical violence. This more generalized outcome measure reflects the concerns of several constituencies involved both in the emergence of battered women as a public policy issue and the development of programs, services and legislation to protect victims. Post-project *violence*, on the other hand, refers to physical acts of violence, which often are the criteria prescribing certain types of legal sanctions against the assailant.

To determine whether restraining orders are effective for different types of clients, two variables are introduced to describe the history of violence in the relationship prior to program intervention: the most serious prior injury, and whether the batterer was violent toward strangers as well as his spouse/partner. These measures of "prior violence" are chosen because of their importance to police or court actions in domestic violence cases. The most serious prior injury often influences whether an incident results in arrest and what offense is charged. We used two categories: low severity (bruises or less) and high severity (lacerations or worse). Prior research shows that these injury categories generally correspond to misdemeanor or felony offense classifications. Violence toward strangers as well as spouse/partner is an indicator of the batterer's "general" violence, which in turn may be related to police decisions to arrest, prosecutorial charging decisions, and sentencing.

The assessments rely primarily on contingency analyses to determine the associations among victim and assailant characteristics, services and outcomes. Although these descriptive methods lack the necessary rigor either to infer causality or to generalize to broader populations, this quasi-experimental design resulted in information useful to policy makers and other audiences, and provided interesting depictions of the relationships among the variables. It should be noted that table totals may not sum to 270 because of missing data for certain variables.

RESULTS

Of the 270 victims interviewed, 66 (24%) had obtained restraining orders as a result of their contact with the family violence intervention projects. Twenty-three others (9%) had obtained restraining orders prior to project contact, for a total sample of 89 (33% of those interviewed). An analysis of the victim background characteristics and relationship history shows the attributes of those who seek a restraining order: They are younger, employed women in shorter, less violent marriages, who have a history of prior separations. The presence of children in the home is also associated with receipt of a restraining order.

Overall, there appear to be no particular patterns of victim or offense characteristics to describe who will seek or receive a restraining order. However, the profile above suggests that restraining orders are more useful to those victims who can become fiscally independent through employment, and are less often sought by older women in more violent marriages with longer abuse histories. In other words, restraining orders are more commonly received in cases where the victim has fewer emotional and financial ties to the batterer, or where the prior violence is less severe. Recipients also tend to have previously attempted to escape the violence through separation. Victims who have longer histories of violence, and are financially tied to the assailant, may be less inclined to seek help through a restraining order.

Clients were asked to rate the overall effectiveness of restraining orders, using a four-point Likert-type scale. Slightly over one-fourth (26%) evaluated them as being "not at all effective," and one respondent (2%) said it was "too soon to tell." The remainder reported that restraining orders were either "somewhat effective" (29%) or "very effective" (43%) in terms of avoidance of further abuse and violence.

Overall, post-project abuse and violence are unaffected by the presence of a restraining order (see Tables 1 and 2). Nearly three victims in five were abused within four months regardless of whether they had obtained a restraining order. For post-project violence, the rate is lower: one woman in four was re-victimized, irrespective of the presence of a restraining order.

Previous domestic violence research has shown that interventions may be more effective for certain types of cases. As discussed earlier, our analyses measured the effects of restraining orders for

Table 1

Effects of Restraining Orders on Post-Project Abuse

		Restraining Order In Effect			
		No		Yes	
Post-Project Abuse	No	60	(41%)	39	(44%)
	Yes	97	(59%)	50	(56%)
	Total	165	(59%)	89	(35%)

$(x^2 = .16, p = ns)$

Table 2

Effects of Restraining Orders on Post-Project Violence

		Restraining Order In Effect			
		No		Yes	
Post-Project Violence	No	87	(73%)	39	(76%)
	Yes	33	(27%)	12	(24%)
	Total	120	(70%)	51	(30%)

$(x^2 = .18, p = ns)$

cases with different histories of violence. We examined the relationship between post-project abuse or violence in the presence of a restraining order for clients with differing levels of prior violence histories. The results show that when restraining orders are not in effect, victims are more likely to be abused after project intervention, regardless of the history of pre-project violence. Approximately 59% of all victims who did not receive restraining orders were reabused. Victims who received restraining orders were less likely to be reabused, but only if their prior injuries were less severe. Table 3 shows that 44% of victims with restraining orders with less severe prior injury were reabused, compared to 67% with more severe prior injuries. In other words, restraining orders are likely to be effective in reducing post-project abuse, but only for victims with less severe prior injury. For victims with more severe pre-project injuries, the presence of a restraining order has no effect on post-project abuse. The results are statistically significant. The effects of restraining orders on post-project violence differ from the effects on post-project abuse. The incidence of post-project violence remains the same, regardless of whether a restraining order is in effect and irrespective of the severity of injuries prior to program intervention.

We turn now to a parallel analysis of the effects of restraining orders, this time controlling for the assailants' general violence tendencies. Overall, there is no difference in the rate of post-project abuse for more or less violent men. In other words, victims' post-project abuse remains the same regardless of whether the assailant is violent toward spouses/partners only or toward strangers as well. When the presence of a restraining order is considered, the results change only slightly. Whereas post-project abuse was significantly

Table 3

Post-Project Abuse as a Function of Prior Injury and Presence of a Restraining Order

		Restraining Order In Effect							
		No				Yes			
		Prior Injury				Prior Injury			
		Low		High		Low		High	
Post-Project Abuse	No	43	(46%)	25	(35%)	24	(56%)	15	(33%)
	Yes	50	(54%)	47	(65%)	19	(44%)	31	(67%)
	Total	93	(56%)	72	(44%)	43	(43%)	46	(46%)
		($x^2 = 2.2$, p = ns)				($x^2 = 4.9$, $p < .03$)			

different for low and high prior injury cases, here there is a weak but statistically insignificant effect of restraining orders on post-project abuse (see Table 4). Where assailants are not violent toward strangers, the presence of a restraining order slightly lowers the rate of post-project abuse. Among those assailants who are more violent, that is, also violent towards strangers, the presence of a restraining order has no effect on the rate of reabuse.

As was found in the earlier analysis of post-project violence and prior injury, there is no association between post-project violence and the generality of assailants' violence. That is, post-project violence is not predicted by assailants' general violence tendencies, either in the presence or absence of a restraining order.

These results indicate that while restraining orders are needed and requested by victims in a wide variety of circumstances, they appear to be effective only for less serious cases involving either less severe prior injury or less violent assailants. Restraining orders appear to be more effective in curtailing abuse (including verbal threats and harassment) than physical violence. The rate of violent revictimization among both more or less generally violent assailants is unaffected by the presence of a restraining order. Moreover, the rate of post-project violence is unaffected by the presence of a restraining order, regardless of severity of prior injury. Numerous women who receive restraining orders remain at risk of violence and injury. And, given the prevalence of women with children who utilize restraining orders, their general ineffectiveness in curbing subsequent violence may leave a good number of children at risk for either witnessing violence or becoming assailants or victims themselves. Such a legacy of violence has proven to be a powerful predictor of violence—both stranger and domestic—in future generations.

The strong interaction effects between prior violence (as indicated by most serious prior injury) and the effectiveness of restraining orders certainly deserves further attention, from a clinical as well as from a research perspective. An important subsequent research and analytic task could well involve contrasting jurisdictions in which restraining orders are rigorously enforced versus those in which they receive minimal attention.[22]

SUGGESTIONS FOR IMPROVING THE EFFECTIVENESS OF RESTRAINING ORDERS

Inherent problems in restraining order legislation relate to access limitations, unrealistic procedures and weak sanctions. To mitigate these problems, legislation may be strengthened by amendments, where possible, or completely revised where necessary. Where no restraining order legislation exists, an understanding of these problems will facilitate the enactment of effective statutes.

The definition of abuse must be clear. It should include all conduct which is deemed criminal, including crimes against persons, property and the public. It should include psychological abuse, not only because restraining orders appear effective in preventing psychological abuse but also because of the interrelationship between

Table 4

Post-Project Abuse as a Function of
Extra-Domestic Violence and Presence of a Restraining Order

		Restraining Order In Effect			
		No		Yes	
		Extra-Domestic Violence		Extra-Domestic Violence	
		No	Yes	No	Yes
Post-Project Abuse	No	29 (41%)	32 (44%)	18 (53%)	22 (42%)
	Yes	42 (59%)	41 (56%)	16 (47%)	30 (58%)
	Total	71 (49%)	73 (51%)	34 (40%)	52 (60%)
		(x^2 = .13, p = ns)		(x^2 = .93, p = ns)	

psychological and physical abuse. Although spousal rape is not a crime in all states, it should not be excluded from the definition of abuse for the restraining order.

Legislation should also be amended to eliminate barriers posed by relationship requirements by permitting all persons irrespective of marital status and living arrangements access to restraining orders. Legislation designed exclusively for spouses limits the remedy to only one of several possible relationship types where such protection may be required. Where it is deemed necessary to limit access, restrictions must be realistic. Where states determine that some form of household restriction is necessary, they should permit access in the case of any persons who have lived together, even for a brief period of time. The household limitation should be waived entirely when children are involved.

Procedures should be specifically outlined in the enactment. The following illustrates a model of what should be authorized: 1) no filing fees for obtaining restraining orders; 2) mandatory assistance by the court's clerical personnel in completing and in filing forms; 3) simplified forms; 4) no requirement as to the necessity of having a lawyer; 5) emergency relief available 24 hours a day; 6) child custody and visitation orders which will survive the duration of the restraining order; 7) support orders, both child and spousal; 8) monetary compensation for injuries suffered as a direct result of the abuse; 9) awards of costs and attorneys' fees; and 10) duration of restraining orders for not less than one year.

Provisions relating to enforcement and to sanctions for violation of restraining orders are the weakest areas in current legislation. Statutes should outline procedures relating to arrest and victim assistance. Sanctions should be criminal and not civil. States which currently make violations of restraining orders misdemeanors should consider allowing an election between a misdemeanor or a felony charge in the case of assailants who have already been convicted in the past for such violations. If states wish to retain civil contempt as a sanction, they should at least provide the option of a misdemeanor charge. Criminal charges should be the mandatory sanction in the case of repeated violations, although this may be a case of "too little, too late" in some cases. Finally, provisions should outline the duties of the court and the district attorney in handling restraining order violations.

A slightly different, yet complementary course involves the design and development of comprehensive legislation. Legislation is comprehensive when there is an overall scheme concerning goals and an effective interrelationship of remedies. A battered woman needs legal alternatives. Comprehensive civil and criminal wife battering legislation should facilitate access to remedies and, if wisely designed, may successfully reduce further abuse.

Several states have adopted comprehensive legislation that can serve as models. California provides both civil and criminal remedies. Civil restraining orders may be obtained as part of the Domestic Violence Prevention Act, the Family Law Act, the Uniform Parentage Act, and the harassment statute. Criminal remedies are available under the felony spousal abuse statute and under California Penal Code section 273.5, which makes violation of restraining orders a misdemeanor. California is one of the few states in which a battered woman can recover victim's compensation. Ohio has also adopted civil and criminal restraining order provisions and makes domestic violence a crime. Washington's domestic violence criminal legislation addresses the issues of police response and the duties of the court and the district attorney, and lists numerous crimes in its definition of domestic violence.[23]

The suggestions offered in this paper for improving restraining order legislation and broadening remedies are based on our current knowledge. A deeper understanding of the phenomenon of family violence and of the battered woman's special predicament will promote more effective use of available remedies as well as the development of new, more efficacious ones than presently exist.

We must recognize, at this time, the utility and the limitations of restraining orders. Strengthening existing legislation by increasing access, improving procedures, and imposing criminal sanctions for violations will likely heighten the effectiveness of restraining orders, but only for those seeking "early intervention," where the pattern of violence or injury has not yet escalated. Where it is impossible to amend civil restraining order legislation, an advocacy approach is an alternative method which can be used to implement and enforce existing legislation. Negotiations with courts to improve procedures and enforcement, with law enforcement to ensure appropriate police response, and with the prosecutor's office to improve both interagency coordination and procedures for prosecution illustrate aspects of such an approach. Finally, broadening legislative coverage through the enactment of criminal restraining order provisions and criminal wife beating statutes would afford additional options.

REFERENCES

1. Jeffrey A. Fagan et al., *National Evaluation of the LEAA Family Violence Demonstration Program First Interim Report: History and Development* (San Francisco: The URSA Institute, 1980).
2. Richard J. Gelles, *The Violent Home: A Study of Physical Aggression Between Husbands and Wives* (Beverly Hills, California: Sage, 1974); Murray A. Straus, "Wife-Beating: How Common and Why," in *Family Violence*, ed. J. Eckalaar and J. Katz, (Toronto: Butterworth, 1978); Murray A. Straus, Richard J. Gelles and Suzanne K. Steinmetz, *Behind Closed Doors: Violence in the American Family* (Garden City, New York: Anchor, 1980).
3. Sandra Wexler, "Battered Women and Public Policy," in *Women, Power and Policy*, ed. Ellen Boneparth (New York, New York: Pergamon Press, 1982).
4. Janice L. Grau, "Restraining Order Legislation for Battered Women: A Reassessment," *University of San Francisco Law Review*, 16 1982: 703-41.
5. *Ibid.*
6. *Ibid.*
7. G. Marie Wilt et al., *Domestic Violence and the Police: Studies in Detroit and Kansas City* (Washington, DC: Police Foundation, 1977); Nancy Loving, *Responding to Spouse Abuse and Wife Beating* (Washington, DC: Police Executive Research Forum, 1980).
8. For a complete review of statutes and issues related to access and procedures see Janice Grau, "Restraining Order Legislation for Battered Women."
9. Cf. *ibid.*
10. Cf. *ibid.* See also Lisa Lerman, "Criminal Prosecution of Wife Batterers," *Response*, 4:3 (1981), pp. 1-19.
11. Cf. Jeffrey Fagan et al., *National Evaluation of the LEAA Family Violence Demonstration Program First Interim Report.*
12. Cf. Lisa Lerman, "Criminal Prosecution of Wife Batterers"; Janice Grau, "Restraining Order Legislation for Battered Women."
13. Jeffrey A. Fagan et al., *National Evaluation of the LEAA Family Violence Demonstration Programs Final Report: Volume 1* (San Francisco: The URSA Institute, 1983). See also Janice Grau, "Restraining Order Legislation for Battered Women." One possible explanation for the exclusion of rape is that many states still do not recognize the possibility of rape within marriage.
14. Janice Grau, "Restraining Order Legislation for Battered Women."
15. Cf. Lisa Lerman, "Criminal Prosecution of Wife Batterers."
16. Lenore E. Walker, *The Battered Woman* (New York: Harper & Row, 1979).
17. Janice Grau, "Restraining Order Legislation for Battered Women."
18. *Bruno v. McGuire*, New York Supreme Court, County of New York, Index #21946/76, "Consent Decree."
19. Cf. Nancy Loving, *Responding to Spouse Abuse.*
20. Jeffrey Fagan et al., *National Evaluation of the LEAA Family Violence Demonstration Program Final Report: Volume 1.*
21. Jeffrey Fagan et al., *National Evaluation of the LEAA Family Violence Demonstration Program First Interim Report.*
22. The primary purpose of the research reported in this article was to describe and examine the effects of project services on clients; thorough exploration of the effects of enforcement activities was beyond the scope of the study.
23. Janice Grau, "Restraining Order Legislation for Battered Women."

Domestic Violence in Criminal Court: An Examination of New Legislation in Ohio

Daisy Quarm
Martin D. Schwartz

ABSTRACT. Many states have recently passed new legislation to deal with spouse abuse, including several which have created a new criminal offense: domestic violence. This study examines all 1980 charges under Ohio's new domestic violence law in a large misdemeanor court and concludes that the creation of a new offense category does not cause major changes in measurable court outcomes. For example, 73% of victims who filed charges dropped them before a verdict was reached. This figure is extremely high. Combined with the large number of victims who never file, it suggests that most abusers do not go through a complete trial.

Moreover, even when victims persevere and the batterer is found guilty, very little happens to him. Sixty-four percent did not spend even one day in jail, less than 10% were sentenced to alternative programs, and 27% were neither jailed nor placed on probation. Even when found guilty, most abusers are neither punished nor offered help.

This study makes two recommendations. The first suggests a dual system whereby victims of domestic violence are provided with both criminal and social service alternatives. The second recommendation encourages the courts to experiment with counseling programs for batterers both as a condition for dismissal of charges and as a condition for probation when convicted.

In recent years one of the most active areas of legal change affecting women nationally has been the proliferation of state laws designed to deal with the problem of wife battering.[1] In the past few

---

Daisy Quarm. Department of Sociology. University of Cincinnati. Martin D. Schwartz. Department of Sociology. University of Kentucky. We wish to thank Lee Ellington for her assistance in collecting the data analyzed in this paper.

years, virtually every state legislature has enacted laws designed to deal with some aspect of this social problem, although the specific provisions of these laws differ greatly.[2] States now provide such remedies as temporary or permanent protection orders,[3] the creation of a new criminal offense of domestic violence,[4] the provision of state-funded or state-assisted shelter houses for victims,[5] state-mandated data collection efforts,[6] and increased powers for police to make arrests in misdemeanor assaults.[7]

This proliferation of new laws raises a question: Does it in fact make any difference? Certainly, individual cases can be found where these new powers were helpful, but the question remains as to whether this legislation has had any effect on the problem of wife abuse. It would be a rare person who would claim that new legislation is a panacea for a major social problem, but certainly the logical argument for going to the effort of passing it is to make some difference in the plight of battered women. An alternative, cynical view is that such legal activity is merely "cosmetic window dressing" designed to placate reformers and activists concerned about spousal violence rather than to benefit battered women.[8]

THE DATA

This study examines the effects of an Ohio law which in March, 1979, established the crime of domestic violence and a range of procedures and remedies for the victims of violence caused by family or other household members.[9] This new offense provides that no person "shall knowingly cause or attempt to cause physical harm to any relative, marital partner, or 'person living as a spouse' who resides or has resided with the offender."[10] Violation is a first degree misdemeanor, punishable by a jail or workhouse term of not more than six months, and/or a fine of not more than $1,000. The offense, except for specifying the domestic relationship, is not significantly different from the Ohio statute on assault, also a first degree misdemeanor: "No person shall knowingly cause or attempt to cause physical harm to another."[11]

With the intention of preliminary investigation into the outcomes of cases filed under the new law, data were gathered in one Ohio county with an approximate population of 875,000. This study examines all cases recorded in Hamilton County on the 1980 municipal (misdemeanor) court docket as either domestic violence cases under the new law, or assault cases in which the complainant and the defendant had the same last name and/or address. Additionally, interviews were conducted with court officials, prosecutors, pretrial detention workers, shelter house personnel, crisis line workers, police officers, state training officials, and defense attorneys.

Hamilton County was chosen partially for reasons of data availability, but also because it is a diverse county. Approximately half the population lives in Cincinnati, served by the Cincinnati Police Department and the city prosecutor's office. The other half of the population lives in a wide variety of urban, suburban and rural communities, served by some 44 different police agencies, and mainly represented by the county prosecutor's office.

This study examined only those cases in which formal charges were filed. Of course, a very great number of women do not make complaints to the police after being victimized,[12] and there is wide variation between and within departments in the use of police powers to deal with domestic violence.[13] Since the court in this study handled the criminal misdemeanor charges of some 45 police departments, with prosecution handled both by county and city prosecutors, some variation in the selection of cases by the police and prosecutors occurred. However, the data include a complete population of all charges filed in calendar year 1980, and the major area of interest is the fate of those cases where formal charges were filed. Case records were examined in all cases where docket information was incomplete, but most of the information obtained came from the court docket.

FINDINGS

As can be seen in Table 1, a total of 1458 cases was filed with the court. Of these, 95% involved charges of domestic violence and 5% charges of assault. The new domestic violence law requires that police officers use the domestic violence law when appropriate, since this charge gives the victim access to civil and protective remedies such as temporary protection orders. Where the relationship between the victim and the offender might be doubtful or difficult to prove, police officers are encouraged to use the charge of assault, since failure to substantiate the family or household member relationship could jeopardize the prosecution of a domestic violence

Table 1. Relationship Between the Outcome of the Case and the Charge

Outcome of case	Dom. viol. diff. sex (%)	Assault diff. sex (%)	Dom. viol. same sex (%)	Assault same sex (%)	Other* (%)	All charges (%)	Number of cases
Dismissed, request of prosecuting witness	60.6	43.9	66.7	40.0	0	58.1	(847)
Dismissed, request of prosecuting attorney	3.5	2.7	3.0	11.4	0	3.6	(52)
Dismissed, prosecuting witness didn't show up	13.1	21.9	15.2	31.4	0	14.7	(214)
Dismissed, request of prosecuting witness and prosecuting attorney	0.4	0	3.0	0	0	0.4	(6)
Dismissed, sent to Private Complaints Program	1.4	1.6	0	0	0	1.4	(20)
Dismissed, other reason	0.2	0.5	0	0	0	0.2	(3)
Guilty	10.8	15.5	9.1	11.4	0	11.4	(166)
Not guilty	5.6	7.5	3.0	2.9	100.0	5.8	(84)
Sent to grand jury	0.3	0	0	0	0	0.3	(4)
Open warrant	3.3	4.8	0	2.9	0	3.4	(50)
Other	0.2	0	0	0	0	0.1	(2)
Not ascertained	0.6	1.6	0	0	0	0.7	(10)
TOTAL	100.0	100.0	100.0	100.0	100.0	100.1	(1458)
Number of cases	(1202)	(187)	(33)	(35)	(1)	(1458)	

*Original charge domestic violence, amended to a simple assault.

case.[14] The data collected in this study do not allow us to ascertain whether charges were filed in all cases in which warranted. However, the large number of cases filed does indicate that the new charge of domestic violence is being used.

Although both the assault and domestic violence statutes are written in sex-neutral language, the charges filed are not sex-neutral. In 90% of the cases, the victim was female and the defendant was male; in 5% the victim was male and the defendant was female; and in 5% of the cases the defendant and victim were the same sex.[15]

Dismissed Cases

The new Ohio domestic violence legislation was designed to make "prosecution a viable alternative for a mate suffering physical abuse within the home."[16] Nationally, the most serious impediment to prosecution has always been a combination of dismissed charges, refusal to appear as a witness, or other unwillingness to follow through by the complaining witness. In studies of courts operating under regular assault statutes, investigators have typically found that approximately 80% of all cases of domestic violence are dismissed by the court either at the victim's request or because the victim failed to appear in court.[17]

Under the new Ohio domestic violence law the frequency of dismissed cases is also high. Excluding those cases in which there is an open warrant, one finds that 1142 or 81% of all cases before the court were dismissed. Of these, 1061 or 93% were dismissed either at the request of the victim (prosecuting witness), or because the victim did not show up in court.

The most likely explanation of the high percentage of dismissed cases even with the new legislation is that the new law does not address the reasons for the high dismissal rate. In agreement with studies in other communities, local shelter house workers and crisis line counselors suggest several reasons for the high dismissal rates.

Fear is mentioned as one major reason women drop charges. An unknown number of women drop cases because of threats or fear of reprisal by the offender. While this fear may be common among all victims,[18] there is good reason to believe that it is even more common among domestic violence victims, including the large number of women who are escorted by their attackers when they come in to drop charges.[19]

Victims also find in lengthy delays, inconsistent information, the complexity of the process, and the inconvenience of losing time at work or arranging child care reasons to ask for charges to be dropped. Case delay, when combined with the victim's lack of confidence in the system, may account for many dropped cases.[20]

Prosecutors in the county studied, as is common nationally,[21] attributed the large number of dropped cases to reconciliation between the victim and the offender. Often stated in terms graphic and uncomplimentary to women, the prosecutors' argument is that women use the justice system only in the heat of anger, or else to play a "oneupsmanship" game with their spouses.

This reconciliation hypothesis suffers from an inherent tautology: women who drop charges are presumed to have reconciled with their abusers, and therefore we can attribute most dropped cases to reconciliation. A more useful hypothesis for further investigation is that many battered women suffer from a lack of knowledge about the criminal justice system. Victim assistance workers find that battered women often expect that the justice system will provide no solutions to their problems, which would militate for dropping the case, or that on conviction the system will provide too extreme a penalty for their attackers. Those who argue for pressing criminal charges often fail to consider adequately the position in which this situation places the complainant. A victim often believes that her marriage could not withstand the strain of a husband jailed for perhaps six months on the basis of her testimony, and that a decision to press charges may in fact be a decision to divorce. A hypothesis worthy of further study is the suggestion, by Cincinnati counselors of battered women, that victims who press charges diligently are predominantly those who have come to the conclusion that their marriage is at an end. The position of many experts is that battered women often suffer from feelings of unworthiness, self-doubt, depression and dependence,[22] a state which has even been compared to that of brainwash victims in prisoner-of-war camps.[23]* Perhaps many women, then, find it difficult to take a drastic step, which they perceive as ending their marriages.

Some final reasons to expect large numbers of dropped cases would be the actions of prosecutors and the difficulty of obtaining convictions. Prosecutors throughout the country generally attempt

---

*Such experts may reinforce victimization, in effect blaming the victim, and underestimate the power dynamics of a battering relationship—ED.

to conserve resources and to maximize their conviction rates.[24] When prosecutors attempt to conserve, there may be a self-fulfilling prophecy at work: to the extent prosecutors anticipate that women will drop charges, they may pressure or recommend this early in the process. Given the difficulty of prosecuting a case in which witnesses rarely exist, rarely has evidence been carefully preserved by the police. The offender often seems more self-assured and unflustered than the victim; and prosecutors may encourage dismissed charges as an alternative to losing cases at trial.[25] This study reveals no specific evidence that prosecutors routinely acted in this manner, but the frequency of the suggestion by observers throughout the country makes it a hypothesis worthy of direct study in the future.

Those Who Are Found Guilty

After the attrition due to dismissals and other reasons, a total of 250 cases in Hamilton County proceeded to what most people consider the normal court outcome: a finding of guilty or not guilty. As 1,458 cases were originally filed, only 17.1% reached the final decision point.

Of these 250 cases, 66.4% or 166 persons were found guilty, including both guilty pleas and trials. The figure represents the percentage found guilty by all judges. Table 2 shows that there was considerable variation from judge to judge, with the conviction rate in different courtrooms ranging from 26 to 88%.

Once a finding of guilty has been made, the next issue worth examining is sentencing outcome. In a county which has a strong reputation for harsh sentences, only 35.5% of the 166 guilty defendants served any time at all in jail, including those sentenced to time already served awaiting trial. In addition, Table 2 shows wide variation in sentencing among judges; the percentage of guilty defendants sentenced to jail ranges from 4.3 to 58.3%. A breakdown of the number of jail days actually served is provided in Table 3.

Table 4 examines a suggestion made by several court officials, that judges are more likely in domestic violence cases to use alternative sentences instead of, or in addition to, traditional imprisonment. Such alternative sentences would include mandatory participation in alcohol counseling, other counseling, drug therapy or similar sentences. An order to stay away from the prosecuting witness was not categorized as an alternative sentence.

Despite the fact the law sanctions the use of alternative sentences

Table 2. Conviction Rate and Jailing Rate by Judge

Judge	Total Cases Completed	Conviction	Jail Sentence
A	25	22 (88%)	8 (36%)
B	27	23 (85%)	1 (4%)
C	21	17 (81%)	8 (47%)
D	27	21 (78%)	8 (38%)
E	17	12 (71%)	7 (58%)
F	25	16 (64%)	8 (50%)
G	22	13 (59%)	6 (46%)
H	22	13 (59%)	5 (38%)
I	24	14 (58%)	3 (21%)
J	19	5 (26%)	2 (40%)
All Others	21	10 (48%)	3 (30%)
TOTALS	250	166 (66%)	59 (36%)

Table 3. Number of Jail Days Actually Served by Defendants Found Guilty of Domestic Violence

Number of Days Actually Served	Defendants Found Guilty, Domestic Violence and Assault (%)	Defendants Found Guilty Domestic Violence, Different Sex (%)
0	64.5	65.4
1-5	4.2	4.5
6-10	5.4	4.6
11-15	3.0	3.8
16-30	10.8	10.1
31-60	3.0	2.3
61-90	1.8	1.5
91-188	7.2	7.8
TOTAL	99.9	100.0
(Number of Cases)	(166)	(130)

Table 4. Penalty for Being Found Guilty of Domestic Violence

Penalty	Number	Percent
No alternative sentence,[1] no days jail served	98	59.0
Alternative sentence, no days jail served	9	5.4
No alternative sentence, 1-15 days jail served	19	11.4
Alternative sentence, 1-15 days jail served	2	1.2
No alternative sentence, 16-990 days jail served	33	19.9
Alternative sentence, 16-990 days jail served	5	3.0
TOTAL	166	99.9

[1] Requiring the abuser to stay away from prosecuting witness was not considered an alternative sentence for the purpose of this analysis.

in domestic violence and child abuse cases,[26] less than 10% of all those convicted of domestic violence were given alternative sentences. No relationship between alternative sentences and lack of imprisonment was found. In fact, although the numbers are small, a slightly higher percentage of those receiving incarcerative sentences also received alternative sentences.

As can be seen in Table 5, the most common sentence was probation. Although almost half of all offenders were also fined, Table 6 indicates that fines were usually under $100.

In summary, then, from a total of 1,458 domestic violence cases filed in an entire year, 1142 cases were dropped, 84 defendants were found not guilty, and 166 defendants were found guilty. Only 59 persons (4%) served any time at all in jail, with 39 of these (two/thirds) serving 30 days or less. In only 12 cases, less than 1% of those filed, did the defendant receive a sentence of at least 3 months in jail.

EVALUATION

Any interpretation of these figures depends on the goals proposed for new protective legislation. Dealing, as this study does, with only the adjudicatory and sentencing process precludes any discussion of whether other sections of Ohio's Domestic Violence Act served useful purposes. For example, the act provided police officers with

Table 5. Probation

Time Period on Probation	Defendants Found Guilty, Domestic Violence and Assault (%)	Defendants Found Guilty Domestic Violence, Different Sex (%)
None	33.1	30.8
3 months	.6	.8
6 months	4.8	5.4
1 year	48.2	50.0
2 or more years	13.2	13.1
TOTAL	99.9	100.1
(Number of cases)	(166)	(130)

Table 6. Fines

Amount of Fine	Defendants Found Guilty, Domestic Violence and Assault (%)	Defendants Found Guilty Domestic Violence, Different Sex (%)
$0	50.6	53.1
$1-50	20.5	22.3
$51-100	16.9	11.5
$101-200	4.8	5.4
$201-500	3.0	3.1
More than $500	4.2	4.6
TOTAL	100.0	100.0
(Number of Cases)	(166)	(130)

the power to make arrests immediately after a complaint in a domestic violence misdemeanor case, as compared to the requirement in assault cases (which a police officer did not witness) that the victim first swear out a private complaint and apply for an arrest warrant at the courthouse.

An expected result of legislation such as that passed in Ohio would be an increase in the number of criminal cases reaching the courts. After all, singling out domestic violence as a special crime, particularly as in Ohio where it is coupled with mandatory police training on the subject, would seem likely to increase the number of arrests and prosecutions for the proscribed behavior. Ideally, one would want to examine whether increased court activity on domestic violence lessens the total amount of such violence in society, either through the deterrent effect of the criminal law, or through a more complex process of making such activity less acceptable by changing group norms. Measuring the new law's effect on domestic violence is precluded by lack of data in either the past or the present on the extent of battering in this country. Even the newest data collection efforts capture only a portion of the total incidence of battering, and are presumably not comparable to existent older data on the subject.

A decision to emphasize use of the criminal justice system presumably implies a positive value toward the traditional legal process and outcomes. Reforms promoting mediation, counseling or informal dispute resolution most often divert cases from the criminal courts. A warranted assumption is that a new law promoting criminal courts presumes that these courts are a useful and appropriate means to deal with crimes of domestic violence.

Inquiries into the criminal courts' ability to deal with spouse abuse have not been generally optimistic. Raymond Parnas, for example, suggests that the "traditional judicial process is neither an effective solution nor a deterrent, and in fact can aggravate an inflamed situation."[27] Michael Freeman argues that "the criminal law is a blunt instrument and few women want to use it. This is perfectly understandable. . . sentences are often derisory."[28] Those who have studied the criminal courts agree generally that however good the use of criminal sanctions is theoretically, the usual practice of these courts does little to prevent effective future spouse abuse.[29] Even if the police make arrests, the percentage of dropped cases is extremely high, and prosecutors and judges rarely take such cases seriously.[30] Very few defendants actually go to jail and, as Parnas observes, "the great majority are handled summarily and off-the-cuff. What little innovation is utilized by our courts is frequently and disturbingly extralegal."[31] Thus, the typical argument in the literature typically does not dispute that domestic violence is a serious social problem, but suggests the cases might not belong in the criminal court system because the system has not been effective.

Strong arguments have been made by reformers for increased use of traditional court processes in domestic violence cases. Lobbying efforts have recently been successful in some states in obtaining new laws meant to increase arrests and court cases. To the extent reformers and legislators envisioned the passage of new legislation greatly improving the ability of battered women to convict and jail their attackers, the law must be considered a failure. Unfortunately, a great many factors which might modify this conclusion cannot be studied because information is not available. For example, an important question for further study is the deterrent effect of such legislation. Deterrence studies are generally complex and problematic,[32] but it would be valuable to uncover the deterrent effect on the abuser of the process of beginning a criminal case. It is not uncommonly argued that for some defendants, the process of being arrested, booked, perhaps kept in jail overnight, and arraigned produces all the deterrent effect the law has, and that further processing would not produce greater effects.[33] Certainly it is a common experience that after a criminal charge has been filed, batterers promise their victims that they will stop their abusive behavior in return for dropped charges. A study of the future experiences of women who drop cases could be illuminating.

This study demonstrates that if the goal of new domestic violence legislation is to put large numbers of batterers in jail or prison, the simple addition of a new section of the penal code may not be the answer. In discussing civil commitment procedures, George Dix made a comment that may be relevant to the discussion of new domestic violence legislation. He suggested that attempts to effect social change through legislation are unlikely to succeed unless they also take into account the political demands on the legal system.

> Where there is no readily available alternative means of satisfying these demands, those upon whom the demands are made will, if possible, use the flexibility in the resources available to them to satisfy the demands as best they can. Attempted revisions which neither eliminate the flexibility (which is probably impossible) nor alter the demands are unlikely to have significant effects.... An attempt to alter the function of a system... by simply enacting a restrictive criteria and inserting in the system a judicial officer with directions to apply that criteria (is) destined in advance to failure.[34]

For battered women, legislation which does not address the problems and causes of dropped cases and refusals to prosecute will not produce a major improvement on the current system of simply using assault statutes to prosecute batterers. Since the tendency of the criminal law is always to favor what it considers the more respectable (men) over the less (women),[35] reliance on traditional court processes alone does not seem all that promising. The lower municipal courts seem particularly immune to change through legal mandate. As Malcolm Feeley has noted:

> The lower court is a complex, flexible institution that is able to absorb efforts to change it and adapt to new circumstances without abandoning old ways. Whatever new programs or directions are added to the court will be deflected, adapted, and absorbed in a variety of predictable ways.[36]

Most commentators on the criminal court in domestic violence cases come away questioning the use of the criminal court at all for such cases.[37] These questions, or conclusions, have generally been based on practical considerations, such as whether counseling or mediation cuts costs, reduces processing time, or resolves problem situations more easily.[38] Before coming to such a conclusion, however, it would be wise to specify carefully in advance the ends or goals of domestic violence legislation. If the goal of the law is to preserve marriages, no matter what the social cost, marking case folders closed in the cheapest and quickest possible manner, then diversion from the criminal justice system seems to be the solution. To the extent that one views domestic violence as a marital "dispute," which can be mediated and resolved, then mediation services seem a likely alternative.*

There may be reasons to pass legislation other than the attainment of immediate, short-term gains. Joseph Gusfield, for example, has argued that in addition to instrumental goals such as increasing convictions, law often has symbolic functions. Here the goal may be "public affirmative of a moral norm (which) directs the major institutions of the society to its support."[39] Symbolic laws may also have instrumental functions, in that they might have some success limiting the proscribed behavior; but the primary purpose here is the political statement involved. Since under any circumstances only a very small percentage of law violators will ever receive incarcerative sentences, attempts to mandate small increases in the sentences may have little immediate impact on societal behavior.

Another purpose of criminal law is deterrence, either individual or general. While most people regulate their behavior according to a wide variety of social, personal, and moral values, and some people

---

*For an alternative view see the *Harvard Women's Law Journal* 7 (Spring 1984)—ED.

will violate laws no matter what their content, an unknown percentage of the population will regulate its behavior for no other reason than fear of criminal sanction.[40] Thus, the passage of new laws criminalizing domestic violence may have some unknown deterrent value, even if there is little evidence that criminal courts negatively sanction large numbers of law violators.

Closely tied to the concept of deterrence is the idea of law as an educational device. The publicity given the enactment of domestic violence legislation and the occasional sanctioning of an offender may usefully encourage moral codes against wife beating, by a public statement that such behavior is wrong and should not be tolerated.[41] It may be desirable to have special domestic violence laws in operation as an educational device and a statement on the relative power positions of women and men in society, even if such laws will not substantially increase the number of convictions and incarcerative punishments.

The point remains. No matter what the abstract value of domestic violence legislation, the criminal law does not provide an alternative or solution acceptable to most victims. Given the assumption that in relatively few instances of battering will criminal charges be filed, and the finding that over 80% of filed charges will be dismissed, one can conclude that the criminal justice system provides little effective help or hope for most victims.

Certainly it would be attractive to suggest, as many commentators have, that if one abandons the criminal justice system in favor of some form of mediation and counseling, then at least some attempt at help will be offered to all individuals who currently file charges. Solutions which move all cases to alternative processes at the same time deny some battering victims the protection of the criminal law. As the data in this study show, there remains a very large group (about 20%) of victims who diligently pursue their cases against their attackers to a final court decision. Diversion of all cases would deny these battering victims the protection of the criminal law.

Because it may call into question the purpose of the criminal code, the recommendation for diversion is a difficult one. Once the diversion process has begun, informal procedures could provide resolution for numerous violations outside the criminal court arena. Most acquaintance crime, business crime, white collar crime, and many other events now considered criminal could be processed in informal proceedings, although widespread decriminalization calls into question the maintenance of criminal laws at all except for cases of victimization by total strangers (and there are numerous examples of possible resolution of these events outside court).

A solution preferable to diverting all cases to counseling or mediation is the provision of alternative avenues. This provision would allow the full protection of the criminal law when the individual feels it is in her best interest, but still provide some form of societal help in those cases in which the individual does not wish to pursue criminal proceedings to a conclusion. For example, both counseling treatment programs for batterers and services for victims, such as marriage counseling, divorce counseling or assertiveness training, should be provided. Great care should be taken in the design of such a dual system to avoid discouraging women who wish to press criminal charges from doing so.

Our data indicate that although many receive suspended sentences, most defendants found guilty of domestic violence do not go to jail. Even when an abuser is convicted, he rarely receives either punishment or help. In those cases in which the outcome is conviction, the court should be encouraged to use sentences other than suspended ones. Courts should also be encouraged to experiment with counseling programs designed especially to treat wife beaters both as a condition for dismissal of charges and as a condition of probation for the convicted.

One major roadblock to alternative sentences is that in most areas the services do not exist and providing them would be perceived as additional financial burdens for the courts. Treatment programs for batterers are cheaper than jail sentences, but more expensive than the suspended sentences currently received by most convicted batterers.[42] With the high costs of processing cases, victim services could also be less expensive than regular court processing.

We believe the suggestion that all or almost all cases be diverted from the criminal process is ill-advised. The diversion process could reinforce traditional notions that domestic violence need not be taken seriously. Moreover, most diversion occurs without the provision of a quality alternative. A dual system, whereby victims of domestic violence are provided with both criminal and social service options, is more desirable than the criminal process or diversion process alone. By using a dual system, it might be possible to obtain some of the best of both worlds. Legislation criminalizing battering would serve symbolic and educational functions, including deterrence, as well as send a small number of batterers to jail; the services provided both the batterer and the victim would make inroads, at least in individual cases, toward ending specific instances of domestic violence.

REFERENCES

1. Although some men are battered by their wives and people can be and are battered by children, grandparents, uncles and a wide variety of friends, lovers and relatives, it is widely assumed (and is a premise here) that most abuse and most serious abuse is committed by men against their wives or lovers. As most of the impetus for such laws, as well as most of the support, stems from this premise, it will also be a supposition used in this study.
2. See for example Lisa G. Lerman, "State Legislation on Domestic Violence," *Response* 3 (August/September 1980): 1-16.
3. See for example Me. Rev. Stat. Ann. tit. 19, Sec. 761 to 764; Md. Ann. Code art. 4 Sec. 402(a), 404, 501 to 506; Minn. Stat. Ann. Sec. 518B.01; 42 Pa. Cons. Stat. Ann. R.C.P., Rules 1901 to 1905; Tex. Fam. Code Ann. tit. 4 Sec. 71.01; Vt. Sta. Ann. tit. 19 Sec. 1101 to 1108.
4. See for example, Ark. Stat. Ann. Sec. 41.1653 to 41.1659; Cal. Penal Code Sec. 1000.6 to 1000.11; Haw. Rev. Stat. Sec. 709-906; N.C. Gen. Stat. Sec. 14-134.3, 15A-401, 15A-534; Ohio Rev. Code Ann. Sec. 2919.25-26; R.I. Gen. Laws Sec. 11-5-9; Tenn. Code Ann. Sec. 39-602.
5. See for example Fla. Stat. Ann. Sec. 409.602 to 409.605; La. Rev. Stat. Ann. Sec. 46:2121 to 46:2125; Md. Ann. Code art. 88A Sec. 101 to 105; Mass. Gen. Laws Ann. ch. 18, Sec. 2(a)(14); Wash. Rev. Code Ann. Sec. 70.123.010 to 70.123.900.
6. See for example Iowa Code Sec. 236; Ky. Rev. Stat. Sec. 209.010 to 209.090; Me. Rev. Stat. Ann. tit. 25, Sec. 1544; Mont. Codes Ann. Sec. 40-2-402; N.H. Rev. Stat. Ann. Sec. 106-B; N.Y. Jud. Law Sec. 216(1)(d)-(f).
7. Alaska Stat. Sec. 18.65.510, 18.65.520; Ariz. Rev. Stat. Sec. 13-3602; Mich. Comp. Laws. Ann. Sec. 764.15a, 769.4a; Nev. Rev. Stat. Sec. 171.124; Ch. 178, 1979 N.M. Laws, p. 633; N.D. Cent. Code Sec. 29-01-15(4).
8. Don Campbell, "Battered Wives: Will the New Act Really Help?" *Police Review* 6 (May 1977): 585. See also Laurie Wermuth, "Domestic Violence Reforms: Policing the Private?" *Berkeley Journal of Sociology* 27 (1982): 27-49.
9. Since the literature on police response and social service response to battering are the stronger parts of the domestic violence literature, a decision in this study was made to concentrate on court processes instead.
10. Ohio Rev. Code Ann. Sec. 2919.25.
11. Ohio Rev. Code Ann. 2903.13(A).
12. Susan Schechter, *Women and Male Violence* (Boston: South End Press, 1982), pp. 24-27.
13. *The Federal Response to Domestic Violence* (Washington, D.C.: United States Commission on Civil Rights, 1982), pp. 24-26.
14. Cincinnati Police Training Bulletin No. 123 (March 25, 1979), pp. 2-3.
15. Although most of the discussion on domestic violence focuses on married couples who live together, in only 65% of the cases here did the victim and defendant live at the same address, including those individuals with the same last name (49%) and those with different last names (16%). This information was not available for about eight % of the cases.
16. The Report from the Attorney General's Task Force, p. 17.
17. Lisa G. Lerman, "Criminal Prosecution of Wife Beaters," *Response* 4 (January/February 1981): 2.
18. Lisa Lerman, "Criminal Prosecution," p. 3.
19. Frank J. Cannavale, Jr., and William D. Falcon, *Witness Cooperation* (Lexington, Massachusetts: Lexington Books, 1976), p. 52.

20. Nancy Sieh, "Family Violence: The Prosecutor's Challenge" (unpublished paper), cited in Lisa Lerman, "Criminal Prosecution," p. 2.
21. Lisa Lerman, "Criminal Prosecution," p. 2.
22. See for example Lenore E. Walker, "The Battered Woman Syndrome Study," in *The Dark Side of Families*, ed. David Finkelhar et al. (Beverly Hills: Sage, 1983), pp. 31-48; Jennifer Baker Fleming, *Stopping Wife Abuse* (New York: Anchor Books, 1979); Roger Langley and Richard C. Levy, *Wife-Beating: The Silent Crisis* (New York: Dutton, 1977); Maria Roy, ed., *Battered Women: A Psychosociological Study of Domestic Violence* (New York: Van Nostrand-Reinhold, 1977); Margaret Ball, "Issues of Violence in Family Casework," *Social Casework* 58 (January 1977): 3-12; Bonnie E. Carlson, "Battered Women and their Assailants," *Social Work* 22 (November 1977): 455-60.
23. Suzanne Steinmetz, "Wife Beating: A Critique and Reformulation of Existing Theory," *Bulletin of the American Academy of Psychiatry and the Law* 6 (1978): 322-24.
24. Frank Miller, *Prosecution: The Decision to Charge a Suspect with a Crime* (Boston: Little, Brown, 1969).
25. Dolores J. Trent, "Wife Beating: A Psycho-Legal Analysis," *Case and Comment* 84 (November/December 1979): 22; Del Martin, *Battered Wives* (San Francisco: Glide, 1976), pp. 109-11.
26. Ohio Rev. Code Ann. Sec. 2933.16, which went into effect March 27, 1979, the same day as the new domestic violence statute (2919.25), specifically states that for those persons convicted of 2919.25 (domestic violence) or 2919.22 (endangering children), "the court may suspend execution of sentence and place the offender on probation conditioned upon the participation of the offender, to the satisfaction of the court, in a program of clinically appropriate psychiatric or psychological treatment."
27. Raymond I. Parnas, "Judicial Response to Intra-Family Violence," 54 *Minnesota Law Review* 642 (1970).
28. M. D. A. Freeman, "Violence in the Home: The New Law," 127 *New Law Journal* 159 (February 17, 1977).
29. See for example Susan Maidment, "Law's Response to Marital Violence in England and the U.S.A.," 26 *International and Comparative Law Quarterly* 403-44 (April 1977).
30. See for example Elizabeth Truninger, "Marital Violence: The Legal Solutions," 23 *Hastings Law Journal* 259 (November 1971).
31. Raymond I. Parnas, "Prosecutorial and Judicial Handling of Family Violence," *Criminal Law Bulletin* 9 747-48 (November 1973).
32. Franklin Zimring and Gordon Hawkins, *Deterrence* (Chicago: University of Chicago Press, 1973).
33. Martin D. Schwartz, Todd R. Clear and Lawrence F. Travis III, *Corrections: An Issues Approach* (Cincinnati: Anderson, 1980).
34. George E. Dix, "Acute Psychiatric Hospitalization of the Mentally Ill in the Metropolis: An Empirical Study," *Washington University Law Quarterly* 558 (Fall 1968); see also Edwin M. Lemert, "Legislating Change in the Juvenile Court," *Wisconsin Law Review* 447 (Spring 1976), for the suggestion that "formal structures and procedures can be changed, but old ends persist and continue to be satisfied."
35. Donald Black, *The Behavior of Law* (New York: Academic Press, 1976), pp. 115-20.
36. Malcolm Feeley, *The Process Is the Punishment* (New York: Russell Sage Foundation, 1979), p. 292.
37. See for example, Raymond Parnas, "Judicial Response"; Susan Maidment, "Law's Response"; Elizabeth Truninger, "Marital Violence."
38. F. Dellapa, "Mediation and the Community Dispute Center," in *Battered Women*, ed. Maria Roy.
39. J. R. Gusfield, "On Legislating Morals: The Symbolic Process of Designating Deviance," 56 *California Law Review* 54-72 (1968).
40. Franklin Zimring and Gordon Hawkins, *Deterrence*, pp. 114-15. See also Raymond

1. Parnas, "The Relevance of Criminal Law to Inter-Spousal Violence," in *Family Violence*, ed. John Eckelaer and Sanford Katz (Toronto: Butterworths, 1978).

41. Martin D. Schwartz, "The Spousal Exemption for Marital Rape Prosecution," 7 *Vermont Law Review* 33-57 (Spring 1982).

42. Barbara Star, *Helping the Abuser: Intervening Effectively in Family Violence* (New York: Family Service Association of America, 1983).

PART II:
SEXUAL ASSAULT

Despite the existence of statutes making rape a criminal offense, it remains one of the most underreported crimes. Obstacles to reportage include ineffective legislation which narrowly defines the crime, the statutory requirements of independent corroboration, and laws that permit examination of the character of the victim.

By removing these obstacles recent legislative reforms have attempted to encourage women to report rape. Contributors to this section examine the impact of these reforms. Judith Osborne reviews the Canadian rape law passed in 1975, which attempted to remove impediments to the successful prosecution of alleged rapists. She argues that the intent of the law makers was not accomplished because of the statute's vague language and problems of judicial discretion.

Susan Caringella-MacDonald evaluates the effectiveness of Michigan's 1974 Criminal Sexual Conduct Code by looking at the prosecutor's role in the new law's implementation. She finds that although some problems remain, rigorous prosecutorial action led to decreasing attrition rates. Both Caringella-MacDonald and Osborne observe that legislative intent can be frustrated by those charged with implementing the law.

Rape Law Reform:
The New Cosmetic for Canadian Women

Judith A. Osborne

ABSTRACT. This article offers a review of the changes that have occurred in Canadian rape law since 1975 and of their impact on and implications for Canadian women. These modifications relate to evidence, procedure and substance. The requirement of corroboration has been repealed; new guidelines have been issued for questioning the complainant about her sexual history; and rape has been redefined as sexual assault of varying degrees. This paper argues that experience since 1975 with these matters and with the related issue of the victim's consent has been disappointing: bad drafting and judicial frustration of legislative intent have impeded any meaningful change.

INTRODUCTION

When Canadian criminal law was codified in 1892, the provisions concerning rape mirrored English common law. Forcible rape (hereafter referred to as "rape") could only be committed by sexual intercourse between a male and a female not married to each other, in the absence of the woman's true consent. Only men could be the principals in rape, and only women could be victims.

The status of rape in the *Criminal Code of Canada*[1] was an intriguing one, included as it was in Part IV, "Sexual Offenses, Public Morals and Disorderly Conduct," rather than in Part VI, "Offenses against the Person and Reputation." No classification scheme of human behaviour is ever totally consistent or logical, but it could be argued in this instance that the placement reflects a long-standing, misguided view of the nature of rape, that is, as aberrant sexual behaviour rather than as an act of violence.

Judith A. Osborne, LL.B., M.A., is an instructor in the Department of Criminology, Simon Fraser University, Burnaby, British Columbia.

Substantive and procedural criticisms of the crime of rape have been made sporadically with negligible impact. Not until rape was treated as a critical issue in the 1960s and 1970s by the escalating women's movement was widespread attention directed to it. In general terms, rape was assailed for perpetuating the subordinate position of women in society.[2] Feminist critics pointed out that rape was not defined as an act of violence against the female victim, and that marital ties, no matter how attenuated, excluded rape by definition. Accordingly, rape law reform was strongly advocated. Reportage of rape appeared to be discouraged by police attitudes, responses to the victim, and by the special trial processes which often forced the complainant to defend herself.

English common law has long regarded allegations of rape with a jaundiced eye, preferring independent testimony from a source other than the victim. In addition, the sexual history of the complainant has been viewed as pertinent to the issue of her consent. In 1975 the federal government of Canada, which has exclusive jurisdiction over criminal law and procedure, amended the rules of evidence and procedure peculiar to rape prosecutions. The required warning to the jury of the danger of convicting the accused on the victim's uncorroborated testimony was eliminated; and limitations were placed on questioning the complainant about her sexual activity.[3] Such evidence was to be judicially screened for relevance before it could be heard in open court. Ambiguities in the legislation became evident in subsequent rape prosecutions. Some courts, for example, revived the common law requirement of corroboration. As a result, further amendments were proclaimed on January 1, 1983.[4] These were changes of form rather than substance, directed at making legislative intent more explicit.

Also included in this recent attempt at criminal law reform was the deletion of the term "rape" from the *Criminal Code of Canada*. The term was replaced by a broader, tripartite scheme of sexual assault: simple sexual assault, sexual assault accompanied by actual or threatened violence, and aggravated sexual assault. The intention behind this change was to stress the violent aspects of such behaviour, rather than its sexual nature, and to increase the number of successful prosecutions. Alongside this reformulation of the law was the codification of the common law defense of honest, but mistaken, belief. A person who had a bona fide, albeit erroneous belief that the complainant had consented to the act, lacked the essential requirement of mens rea and should therefore be acquitted.

What follows is a review and evaluation of the impact of these changes on women in Canada. The analysis will trace the evolution of four key issues—corroboration, credibility, the redefinition of rape, and consent—in the years between 1975 and 1983.

CANADIAN WOMEN AND RAPE LAW REFORM

Over the past decade, Canadian rape law has been the subject of debate in public, political and legal forums, and had been found lacking on both procedural and substantive grounds. Rape, per se, covered only a narrow range of behaviour, occurring between a male and a non-consenting female who was not his spouse. The testimony of a rape victim was treated with scepticism and reserve. Parallels were drawn between her testimony and the evidence of accomplices. The evidence she gave was rarely sufficient, and her credibility could be further impugned by evidence of her prior sexual conduct. As a result, a significant number of rape victims were reluctant to involve themselves in a prosecution. Legislative attention was initially directed to these procedural and evidentiary matters.

Corroboration

Women who make allegations of rape have long been regarded with suspicion by the criminal justice system. A Canadian appeal court judge recently urged trial judges to recognize that rape is easy to allege but difficult to disprove. In addition, the motive for a false accusation is frequently indiscernible.[5] An explicit statement of distrust of complainants of rape appears in a report of the influential English Criminal Law Revision Committee, where a common comparison is drawn between complainants in sexual cases and accomplices to a crime.[6]

> In sexual cases it is the danger that the complainant may have made a false accusation owing to sexual neurosis, jealousy, fantasy, spite or a girl's [sic] refusal to admit that she consented to an act of which she is now ashamed. In the case of an accomplice any special danger that there may be in relying on the witness's evidence is apparent from the fact that he is an accomplice or it can be easily made apparent by the defence. In the case of a sexual offence the danger may be hidden.

This comparison of the complainant in a sexual offense case and an accomplice is one frequently made but unfortunate and unfair, reflecting as it does the tendency to see the complainant in these cases as on trial.

The possibility of fabrication doutbless exists among victims of other types of crime, for example, where insured property is involved. There are specific provisions in the *Code* designed to deal with this possibility. Section 128 makes it a public mischief intentionally to give a false statement accusing some other person of having committed an offence; s.125 prohibits the fabrication of anything with the intent that it be used as evidence in any existing or proposed court proceeding; and s.120 defines the crime of perjury. These provisions apart, what of the fundamental requirement that the Crown must prove its case beyond a reasonable doubt? If doubt does exist as to the veracity of the complaint of rape, is this standard of proof not sufficient to prevent wrongful conviction? Moreover, there is evidence to suggest that rape complaints exhibiting any sign of weakness are screened our prior to the trial.[7]

According to the federal agency, Statistics Canada, there were 3,625 reported rapes in Canada in 1981. The police dismissed 1,066 of them (29.4%) as unfounded.[8] In the face of police inaction, the woman can lay an information before a Justice of the Peace, but this initiative may be blocked by the Crown Attorney refusing to allow the prosecution to proceed. In addition, there are practical difficulties involved in pressing charges without official cooperation. The Crown Attorney also possesses a broad discretion to drop the charges in those cases where the police have seen fit to proceed.

It can be argued quite strongly that there are more than adequate mechanisms available to prevent wrongful convictions in rape cases. Nonetheless, prior to April, 1976, s.142 of the *Code* contained an additional safeguard. This provision required that a corroborative warning be given a jury when the only evidence implicating the accused was the uncorroborated testimony of the complainant. In her study of corroboration in Canada law, Audrey Wakeling observes that the complexity of the caution may have impeded rather than assisted jurors in making a sound judgment based on the evidence. Further, there was a significant potential for error in instructing the jury on this matter, leading to technical appeals.[9] These legal criticisms aside, empirical research has not verified the belief that juries convict hastily on the emotion-laden testimony of alleged rape victims. In their seminal work on criminal juries, Harry Kalven and Hans Zeisel found that jurors view rape charges with great suspicion, rarely returning convictions unless aggravating circumstances, such as visible signs of violence, are present.[10]

The legislative erasure of the corroborative warning was clearly addressed to remedying these defects.[11] All mention of corroboration was removed from s.142, which was then devoted solely to restrictions on questioning the complainant about her sexual history, as will be discussed below. Unfortunately, statutory silence did not settle the issue. Faced with the absence of clear wording that a corroborative warning would no longer be required in rape cases, legal practitioners questioned whether the common law requirement of a warning had been revived. The decision of the Ontario Court of Appeal in *R. v. P.*[12] found a measure of acceptance. Holding that the repeal of s.142 did not restore the common law on the corroboration issue, the Court went on to state that neither did it limit the discretion of the trial judge. In appropriate instances, he might caution the jury in straightforward language as to the risk of relying on the evidence of a single witness without, however, using the term "corroboration."[13] In a subsequent decision of that Court, *R. v. Camp*,[14] it was observed that a judge would actually be under a duty in some cases to warn the jury in simple language as to the risk of relying solely on the evidence of a single witness. Further, he should explain to them the reasons for the necessity for such a caution.

The courts of British Columbia took a different view. The provincial Chief Justice had this to say[15]:

> The judicial resurrection of the former common law rule in respect of cases within the terms of s.142 would, in my opinion, frustrate the parliamentary intent. Parliament made it clear, it seems to me, that cases formerly within s.142 which required a special charge or corroboration were hereafter to be treated as other criminal offences in respect of which no special charge was obligatory.

This statement contrasts with the position of the appellate court in Quebec which recently described the requirement of corroboration as "a rule of good sense" albeit not a rule of law.[16] Finally, in the Ontario case *R. v. Smith*,[17] it was held that, once given, a warning of the danger of convicting on the complainant's evidence could not be undermined by independent support falling short of corroboration. Authority for this decision was drawn from the law of accomplice evidence.[18]

On the basis of these decisions it can be concluded that, while there was no longer any statutory requirement of a corroborative warning in cases relying solely on the evidence of the complainant, judges were instead directed to use their discretion in the matter. Whether they exercised it wisely is impossible to determine objectively. There was certainly no evidence to suggest that judges warned juries of the dangers involved any less frequently than they did before 1976.[19] What is apparent is that reliance was still placed on the law relating to accomplice evidence in order to determine the scope of the revised rules of evidence in rape prosecutions.

In the face of judicial reluctance to accord the 1975 amendment any real effectiveness, Parliament had to be much more explicit. Amending legislation passed at the end of 1982 and brought into operation on the first day of 1983 inserted s.246.4 into the *Code*. This provision specifies that, where an accused is charged inter alia with sexual assault, no corroboration is required for a conviction and further still, "the judge shall not instruct the jury that it is unsafe to find the accused guilty in the absence of corroboration." Hopefully this will settle the matter so that the complainant's evidence will be assessed in accordance with the standard of credibility rather than that of corroboration.

Credibility

The issue of the victim's credibility has not been without its own problems. In particular, evidence of a dubious sexual history almost inevitably tainted the quality of her testimony. Another component of the 1975 revision of s.142 was directed to this issue. Given its more explicit nature, this revision attracted more attention and kudos than the corroboration question.

In short, the new provision set out guidelines for questioning the alleged rape victim about her past sexual history. Before this change was enacted she could be asked questions in open court about her prior sexual conduct, but she could not be compelled to answer by the accused, nor could he lead evidence to contradict her testimony. The leading Canadian case on the prior law indicates, however, that the judge had a discretion to compel an answer.[20] The rationale for this practice rested on a highly questionable assumption:

> If she admitted such sexual relations this went to her credibility no doubt on the ground that a woman whose morals were such that she indulged in sexual activity was less believable. It may

well have been in the 19th century and some time in the 20th century that if a woman indulged in extramarital sex it could be thought that made her a less reliable witness as it reflects on her credit generally.[21]

As Christine Boyle notes, concern grew that the freedom to question the complainant on this collateral issue was being abused, causing humiliation and embarrassment and generally discouraging the reporting of rape incidents.[22] Consequently, s.142, as amended in 1975, provided that there could be no questioning of the complainant as to her sexual conduct with persons other than the accused unless

 a) reasonable notice was given
 b) along with sufficient particulars of the evidence sought to be adduced, and
 c) the judge had decided, after an *in camera* hearing, that its exclusion would prevent the "just determination of an issue of fact in the proceedings, including the credibility of the complainant."

On the face of it, this appeared to be a significant step toward limiting harrassment of complainants on the witness stand. Subsequent judicial elucidation of the provision, however, would suggest that the changes were more apparent than real. Coming as it did from the Supreme Court of Canada, the key case was an unquestionably authoritative decision. In *Forsythe* v. *The Queen*[23] the judgment of the Court was delivered by Chief Justice Laskin, who gave the following interpretation of the terms of s.142. First, and most importantly, it reversed the prior law which entitled an accused from seeking to contradict a denial by a complainant of "sexual misconduct" with others. Further, the defence was not limited to cross-examining the complainant to contradict the denial but could put forward other witnesses to impugn her credibility.[24] This interpretation was viewed by the Court as maintaining a balance between the victim and the accused. She could be relieved of the embarrassment of answering questions about her sexual history in open court but, if the trial judge was of the opinion that her prior sexual activity was relevant, the accused was entitled to an answer to his questions. Second, the complainant was made a compellable witness at the *in camera* hearing on the basis of which the judge decided whether the questions could be asked in open court.[25]

The trade-off implicit in this interpretation of s.142 begs the question whether it represented any real improvement in the position of rape complainants at the trial of their aggressors. The position prior to January 1, 1983, appears to be this: the judge had a discretion to protect the complainant from some or all questioning about her sexual history, but the accused could then insist on answers to this line of questioning and lead evidence to contradict her testimony. As Boyle observes, the complainant's compellability at the *in camera* hearing "involves at least a theoretical reduction in the right of the witness to protect her privacy."[26]

As a result of the interpretation handed down in *Forsythe*, therefore, s.142 as amended simply confirmed the discretion that judges have always had in deciding which questions to allow.[27] At the same time, it eroded the complainant's right not to answer certain questions or be cross-examined on her answers by the defense. Once again, legislative intent and judicial interpretation were at odds. This is partly due to the wording of s.142(1)(b) which indicates the judge must be "satisfied that the weight of the evidence is such that to exclude it would prevent the making of a just determination of an issue of fact in the proceedings, including the credibility of the complainant." Traditionally, however, evidence of past sexual experience went to credibility only, and credibility has not been viewed as a "fact in issue." The Court glossed over this confusion, preferring to base its decision on the less tangible factor of the balance between accused and victim.

The extent of the protection afforded the complainant by s.142 was again considered by the Supreme Court of Canada in *R. v. Konkin*.[28] The four-three majority decision held that evidence of post-offense promiscuity could not be rendered inadmissible as a matter of principle. At trial, an *in camera* hearing had been held in accordance with s.142. The complainant admitted not only several incidents prior to the offense but also a number subsequent to it. In particular, she engaged in sex with five men in one evening and with multiple partners on other occasions. Her explanation was that the trauma of the sexual assault had produced a character change leading to promiscuous behaviour. The trial judge permitted cross-examination on the incidents prior to the offense but not with respect to those following it. On appeal Chief Justice Laskin, speaking for the majority, ruled that such evidence would be admissible if it were needed to ensure a fair trial. In other words, "sexual conduct" may include pre- and post-offense behaviour, depending on the circumstances of the case.

This latter ruling was unaffected by the most recent amendments to sexual offense legislation, passed in 1982, becoming effective January 1, 1983. Included in this latest revision of the *Code* is the repeal of s.142 and the substitution of s.246.6, set out in part below:

> 246.6 (1) In proceedings in respect of an offense under section 246.1, 246.2 or 246.3, no evidence shall be adduced by or on behalf of the accused concerning the sexual activity of the complainant with any person other than the accused unless
>
> > (a) it is evidence that rebuts evidence of the complainant's sexual activity or absence thereof that was previously adduced by the prosecution;
> >
> > (b) it is evidence of specific instances of the complainant's sexual activity tending to establish the identity of the person who had sexual contact with the complainant on the occasion set out in the charge; or
> >
> > (c) it is evidence relating to the consent that the accused al-alleges he believed was given by the complainant to the sexual activity that is the subject-matter of the charge.
>
> (2) No evidence is admissible under paragraph (1)(c) unless
>
> > (a) reasonable notice in writing has been given to the prosecutor by or on behalf of the accused of his intention to adduce the evidence together with particulars of the evidence sought to be adduced; and
> >
> > (b) a copy of the notice has been filed with the clerk of the court.
>
> (3) No evidence is admissible under sub-section (1) unless the judge, magistrate or justice after holding a hearing in which the jury and the members of the public are excluded and in which the complainant is not a compellable witness, is satisfied that the requirements of this section are met.

The general term "sexual activity" is retained. Therefore, on the basis of *Konkin*, it can include encounters before and after the alleged assault.

Another point to note is that the amendment marks a departure from common law principles which categorize the woman's sexual conduct as irrelevant to the issue of consent, collateral only, and going solely to credibility. Now, evidence of her sexual activity may be adduced (subject to the judge's discretion) if it relates to the issue of consent. From being a collateral issue, it has been promoted to the status of relevance to consent.

Redefinition of Rape

In addition to the procedural changes discussed above, the amendments to the *Code* in 1982 make important substantive changes in the law of rape. In order to encourage more successful prosecutions, a tripartite scheme of sexual assault has replaced the narrower crime of rape. Unlike rape, "sexual assault" is not confined to male-female behaviour with emphasis placed on penetration. Three degrees of sexual assault have been created with penalties scaled to the seriousness of the offense:

1. simple sexual assault (s.246.1) carrying a maximum penalty of 10 years' imprisonment;
2. sexual assault along with the possession, use or threatened use of a weapon, threats to a third party or the causing of bodily harm, with a maximum term of 14 years' incarceration, and
3. aggravated sexual assault which has a potential life sentence.[29]

This generic offense applies to "any person"; no mention is made of the marital exemption; and sexual assault is firmly located in Part VI of the Code pertaining to offenses against the person.

As Duncan Chappell notes, the idea of dividing the crime of rape into degrees, with appropriate penalties for each depending on the gravity of the offense, was initially propounded in the United States Model Penal Code in the early 1960s.[30] Growing support for such a scheme in Canadian criminal law followed the 1977 publication of Lorenne Clark's and Debra Lewis's influential work, *Rape: The Price of Coercive Sexuality*, which recommended the deletion of rape from the "Sexual Offenses" section of the *Code* and the creation of new assault offenses.[31] Late the following year, the federal law reform body submitted a report to Parliament, along with draft legislation.[32]

> Our consultations have confirmed that the predominant legal and behavioural characteristic of rape is not for the offender its sexual but rather its aggressive aspect, its violation of the

physical integrity of the human person. In the Commission's opinion the law should reflect this reality.[33]

To this end the Law Reform Commission advocated the creation of two types of prohibited sexual conduct: sexual interference and sexual aggression.[34]

Parliament ultimately chose to adopt a scheme of offenses centered around the concept of sexual assault. The three grades of sexual assault are differentiated by the degree of violence used or threatened and the risk to the victim, rather than by the nature and extent of sexual intimacy. Maximum sentences escalate accordingly. The rationality inherent in this structure is appealing. It may also be illusory as the definition of "sexual assault" is left wide open. The courts will face the task of establishing its parameters.

"Assault" is defined in the revised s.244(1), which is made applicable to sexual assaults by virtue of s.244(2). The definition covers the intentional application of direct or indirect force in the absence of consent; the threatened use of force; and also accosting, impeding or begging while openly in possession of a real or imitation weapon. Consent obtained by force, threats, fraud or the exercise of authority is not true consent (s.244(3)), and will not satisfy the terms of the section. That is as far as the definition of sexual assault goes. There is no clarification as to the factors that will transform assault into sexual assault. A liberal definition would encompass a wide variety of sexual activity; a narrow approach such as that found in the traditional definition of rape would effectively limit the scope of law reforms to a mere change in terminology. Whether the courts choose either of these options or pursue a middle ground remains to be seen.

Consent

Almost by definition, consent, or the lack thereof, has been the focal point of most rape trials. Mens rea is a necessary prerequisite for criminal responsibility. For rape, to establish mens rea required that the man intend to have sexual intercourse with a person whom he is aware is not his wife, knowing that she is not consenting. The requirement of real consent is retained in relation to sexual assault.[35] Unless the accused denies that he was involved in the incident at all, his defense usually alleges the victim's consent, real or apparent.

The causal connection posited between a woman's sexual history, her credibility and her consent has already been discussed. The more recent controversy surrounding the issue of consent is the effect of the accused's honest, albeit mistaken belief that the complainant was a willing partner. The decision of the House of Lords in *Morgan* v. *D.P.P.*[36] ignited a heated debate. A majority of the Law Lords held that an honest but mistaken belief about consent would be a valid defense to a charge of rape. In 1980, the Supreme Court of Canada was confronted with the same issue in *Pappajohn* v. *The Queen*.[37] The Court decided the case in a manner consistent with the English counterpart: an honest, mistaken belief can be a valid defense to a rape charge even if it is also an unreasonable one.

This is a position compatible with the fundamental principles of criminal responsibility. There must be a criminal act (actus reus) coexisting with a guilty mind (mens rea). While a mistake of law will not excuse criminal responsibility, a mistake of fact may be a justifiable excuse. Provided the accused's behaviour would not have been criminal if the facts were as he believed them to be, he will have a valid defense. In cases of rape (and now sexual assault), this generally means the defense will endeavour to prove that the accused believed the woman had given her consent. He made a mistake and did not have the requisite state of mind necessary to establish culpability. In *Pappajohn*, the accused maintained that the complainant had been a willing partner throughout. When, in fact, she became hysterical, he claimed he left the room. He appealed his conviction as far as the Supreme Court of Canada on the grounds that the trial judge should have allowed the defense of honest, mistaken belief to be put before the jury. A majority of the Court agreed that this defense was available, but only if there was evidence available to support it.

Contrary to public opinion, this decision did not reflect the chauvinistic, misguided learnings of an all-male Supreme Court. Rather, it reiterates the fundamental precepts of a system of criminal law based on subjectively ascertained blameworthiness. With relatively few exceptions, criminal responsibility depends on the *accused's* actual state of mind, not on that of the objective reasonable man. As Ken Garley remarks, the Supreme Court simply endorsed the subjective approach to guilt.[38] The Court did not deny that the reasonableness of the accused's belief had a role to play, but solely in relation to credibility. The more unreasonable the accused's belief, the less likely it is that the jury will believe him.[39] In addition, the issue would not even be put to the jury unless there was sufficient evidence available to make it a live issue.[40]

Consistency with principle notwithstanding, criticism of the Court's decision abounded.[41] The substantive law upheld in *Pappajohn* paid the price for the deficiencies of judicial and legislative mishandling of procedural and evidentiary issues. Judged on its own merits, however, the decision was an eminently reasonable one. The judgment of Mr. Justice Dickson illustrates this most clearly. He acknowledges the danger inherent in the defense that rapists could too easily escape conviction simply by alleging the complainant was a willing partner. Nonetheless, this has to be balanced against the fact that there would have to be an evidentiary basis to lend credence to such a claim before a trial judge would allow the defense to be put before a jury. Further, to import the objective standard of the reasonable man into determinations of criminal responsibility would create confusion and inconsistency into the law.[42]

One commentator has suggested that a sensible way to allay fears from the female community that *Pappajohn* constitutes a "rapists' Charter" is by amending the *Code* to enable the trial judge to instruct the jury in a rape case that it can take into account the reasonableness of the accused's mistake in determining his honesty, but not in determining his criminal responsibility.[43] In other words, there would be statutory recognition of judicial practice as outlined in *Pappajohn*. It was further suggested that "if it proves absolutely necessary, a new statutory offense can be created. The offense, specifically, would be having sexual intercourse while being negligent as to the woman's consent."[44]

Parliament has not gone as far as creating a new offense based on negligence, but it has incorporated into recent amendments a subsection s.244(4), dealing specifically with the defense of honest but mistaken belief:

> Where an accused alleges that he believed that the complainant consented to the conduct that is the subject-matter of the charge, a judge, if satisfied that there is sufficient evidence and that, if believed by the jury, the evidence would constitute a defence, shall instruct the jury, when reviewing all the evidence relating to the determination of the honesty of the accused's belief, to consider the presence or absence of reasonable grounds for that belief.

Logically speaking, this provision is not strictly necessary as it simply accords with fundamental principles of criminal law. In this instance, Parliament judged it wiser to be explicit to clarify the issue of consent raised in *Pappajohn*. Two Vancouver criminal lawyers recently observed that the consent amendment was clearly dictated by feminist outrage over the *Pappajohn* case.[45] Nonetheless, the amendment merely represents a restatement of *Pappajohn*. This is evident when one compares s.244(4) to the following quotations drawn directly from that decision:

> The reasonableness, or otherwise, of the accused's belief is only evidence for or against the view that the belief was actually held and that the intent was therefore lacking;[46] and it is not every case of rape in which the accused asserts that the victim was consenting that requires the trial judge to leave this defence to the jury. As with other defences there must be in the evidence some basis upon which the defence can rest, some evidence to convey a sense of reality to the defence [which] . . . must appear from, or be supported by, sources other than the accused in order to give it an air of reality.[47]

CONCLUSIONS

The legislative restatement of the *Pappajohn* decision is not necessarily undesirable, although its placatory undertones could be viewed in a paternalistic light. Indeed, the restatement may serve a positive, clarifying function, but it may also have some damaging side effects. Changes made in the *Code* which do not actually achieve their ostensible aims have been a recurring feature of rape law reform:

1. from 1976-1982 the requirement of corroboration was removed in name only;
2. the sexual history of the complainant, although ostensibly eliminated, remains a-relevant issue;
3. the redefinition of rape as sexual assault in the absence of any discrete criteria may be a case of "a rose by any other name" and
4. honest, mistaken belief as to the victim's consent is still an available defence, with reasonableness relating only to credibility.

As the legal realists indicated decades ago, the judiciary possesses extensive law-making skills. It does not simply apply the law. The real impact of legislative change depends on how it is interpreted or applied in practice. On the one hand, this state of affairs provides the flexibility which enables the law to adapt to time and circumstance. On the other hand, it can also accommodate judicial conservatism. Law making by the legislature or the judiciary is a dynamic process, but it does not inevitably produce change.

Expecting real gains in the short term may be unreasonable given the long-standing myths and prejudices underlying the law's treatment of sexual offenses, but as Chappell observes, the long range outlook for the improved status of women may be more positive: "In this context legal labels and penalties are of far lesser significance than legal behaviours," which may change with time and public debate.[48] A discouraging possibility does exist. The legal profession and more importantly, the judiciary will doubtless recognize the "new" reasonable belief provision for what it is—a cosmetic change—and interpret other provisions of the 1982 revision in the same light. This would be disappointing but no great surprise, given the recent history of rape law reform in Canada.

REFERENCES

1. R.S.C. 1970 c. C-34, s.143.
2. Susan Brownmiller, *Against Our Will: Men, Women & Rape* (New York: Simon & Schuster, 1975); Lorenne Clark and Debra Lewis, *Rape: The Price of Coercive Sexuality* (Toronto: The Women's Press, 1977).
3. *Criminal Code Amendment Act*, 1975, c.93, proclaimed in force April 26, 1976.
4. *Criminal Code Amendment Act*, 1982 (Bill C-127), proclaimed in force January 1, 1983.
5. *R. v. Konkin*, (1982) 63 C.C.C. (2d) 193 (Alta. C.A.) per McGillivray C.J.A. at 199.
6. Criminal Law Revision Committee, *Eleventh Report on Evidence* (London: H.M.S.O., 1972).
7. For a discussion of rape reporting and charging data see L. Clark and D. Lewis, *Rape*, fn. 2 at pp. 57-60; W. Loh, "The Impact of Common Law and Rape Reform Statutes on Prosecution: An Empirical Study," 55 *University of Washington Law Review* 543 (1980).
8. As cited in "Police Mishandle Rape," *Vancouver Province*, October 10, 1982, B1.
9. Audrey Wakeling, *Corroboration in Canadian Law* (Toronto: Carswell, 1977), 122.
10. H. Kalven and H. Zeisel, "The Rape Corroboration Requirement: Repeal Not Reform," 81 *Yale Law Journal* 1379 (1972). See also S.H. Nelson, "An Empirical Study of Jury Decisions in Rape Trials," 1 *Criminal Reports* (3d) 265 (1982).
11. *Criminal Code Amendment Act*, 1975, supra fn. 3, s.8.
12. *R. v. P.*, (1978) 39 C.C.C. (2d) 129 (Ont. C.A.)
13. *Ibid.*
14. *R. v. Camp*, (1977) 36 C.C.C. (2d) 511 at 521.
15. *R. v. Firkins*, (1977) 37 C.C.C. (2d) 227 at 233. (B.C.C.A.).
16. *R. v. Chenier*, (1982), 63 C.C.C. (2d) 36 (Queb. C.A.).
17. *R. v. Smith*, (1982), 66 C.C.C. (2d) 193 (Ont. C.A.).

18. *Ibid.* at 194 per Brooke J.A.
19. Australian studies cited by Duncan Chappell suggest that, despite the presence of new procedural and evidentiary requirements, judicial practice remains largely unchanged ("The Impact of Rape Reform Legislation: Some Comparative Trends," paper presented to the annual meetings of the American Society of Criminology, Toronto, 1982).
20. *Laliberte v. The Queen*, (1877), 15 C.R. 117.
21. *R. v. Konkin, supra* fn. 5 at 197.
22. Christine Boyle, "Section 142 of the Criminal Code: A Trojan Horse?" 23 *Criminal Law Quarterly* 255 (1981).
23. *Forsythe v. The Queen*, (1980) 53 C.C.C. (2d) 225 (S.C.C.)
24. *Ibid.* at 231.
25. *Ibid.* at 235.
26. Christine Boyle, "Section 142," fn. 22 at 257.
27. *Ibid.* See also Neil Brooks, "Rape and the Laws of Evidence," 23 *Chitty's Law Journal* 5 (1975).
28. Unreported decision of S.C.C. delivered April 26, 1983.
29. *Criminal Code Amendment Act*, 1982.
30. D. Chappell, "Impact of Rape Reform Legislation," fn. 19 at 3.
31. L. Clark and D. Lewis, *Rape*, fn. 7 at 185-86.
32. Law Reform Commission of Canada, *Report No. 10: Sexual Offences* (Ottawa: Supply and Services, 1978.)
33. *Ibid.* at 12.
34. *Ibid.* at 13.
35. Subsection 244(3)
36. 1 *Criminal Appeal Reports* 136 (1975)
37. (1980) 52 C.C.C. (2d) 481 (S.C.C.)
38. Ken Garley, *The Law of Rape in Canada: A Critical Analysis of its Shortcomings with Suggestions for Reform* (Unpublished honours thesis, Department of Criminology, Simon Fraser University), at 60.
39. *Pappajohn v. The Queen*, fn. 37 at 492 per Dickson J.
40. *Ibid.* at 481 per McIntyre J.
41. For example Toni Pickard, "Culpable Mistakes and Rape: Harsh Words on Pappajohn," 30 *University of Toronto Law Journal* 415 (1980).
42. *Pappajohn v. The Queen*, for 37 at 498-99 per Dickson J.
43. Ken Garley, *The Law of Rape*, fn. 38 at 66.
44. *Ibid.*
45. L. Still, "The New Rape Laws," *Vancouver Sun*, January 6, 1983, B1.
46. *Pappajohn v. The Queen*, fn. 37 at 482 per Dickson J.
47. *Ibid.* at 481-82 per McIntyre J.
48. D. Chappell, "Impact of Rape Reform Legislation," fn. 19 at 15.

Sexual Assault Prosecution: An Examination of Model Rape Legislation in Michigan

Susan Caringella-MacDonald

ABSTRACT. Since the mid-1970s virtually every state has altered its rape legislation in an effort to rectify problems in the prosecution of such crimes. Because implementation of rape reform statutes can affect the success of these efforts, and because prosecutors play a decisive role in the process, this study assesses one aspect of the effectiveness of reform rape legislation by measuring attrition and conviction rates in the prosecution of sexual assault. Attrition rates in one Michigan jurisdiction operating under the model Criminal Sexual Conduct Code are discussed and then compared to other research data. This comparative examination indicates that the law can be productively employed to combat problems, such as high attrition and low conviction rates, historically associated with prosecution of sexual assault offenses. It is also noted that problems may persist despite reform legislation. For instance, while attrition and conviction rates in this research jurisdiction compared favorably to all other available data, almost two-thirds (64%) of the criminal sexual conduct cases brought to prosecutors were lost at some stage in the criminal justice system. While legislative alterations represent a step in the direction of progress, such measures alone will fall short of generating the encompassing social change necessary to rectify the inequitable treatment of rape victims.

INTRODUCTION

A recent concern in the literature on rape has centered on the problems surrounding prosecution of this crime. Both the carnal

---

Department of Sociology, Western Michigan University, Kalamazoo, Michigan 49008. Gratitude is expressed to James Gregart, Prosecuting Attorney of Kalamazoo County, for his continued support via data access, but more importantly, for his commitment to the victims of sexual assault.

knowledge statutes and the myths underscoring such laws have been challenged.[1] Critics have commented on the double victimization of rape victims by first the sexual assault and then the criminal justice system. The definition of rape as carnal knowledge of a female, forcibly and against her will, has brought about unique case treatment evidenced in corroboration requirements, consent and resistance standards, and the admissibility of victim character evidence. The misguided beliefs which serve as justification for unique standards and treatment of rape revolve around notions of false accusation, victim precipitation, consent, and the predilection of the judicial system to sympathize with victims and thereby convict allegedly innocent men.[2]

These types of beliefs have contributed to high attrition and low conviction rates at all stages of the criminal justice system. Rape is the most underreported offense in the country.[3] Additionally, 15% of the cases coming to the authorities' attention are declared unfounded by police.[4] Of cases reported and founded, 52% are not cleared;[5] and of those reported, founded and cleared, 48% result in the accused rapists' release through acquittals.[6] Other sources indicate that the attrition of rape cases is in fact as high as a 97% loss between report and conviction.[7]

Attrition presents problems other than low conviction rates. It both originates in and leads to the perpetuation of myths and differential treatment of rape cases as compared to all other crimes. For example, beliefs that victims frequently ask for the assault, falsely accuse men, and so forth, relate historically to attrition and acquittal. Conversely, dropping cases has often been viewed as proof that rape victims deserved or consented to the sexual attack. Attrition and nonconviction have, then, operated to sustain myths and to justify strict and unique legal requirements. Because of this circumstance, victims of rape deciding to pursue cases through legal channels have faced discrimination by and trauma from excessive scrutiny of their behavior, credibility, demeanor, resistance, and provocation. The net effect has been to shift the burden in rape cases from demonstrating the offender's guilt to demonstrating the victim's innocence.

By 1980, in direct response to these problems, most states reformed their rape laws.[8] Much of this legislation was meant to eliminate unjust and discriminatory treatment of rape victims. A brief discussion of the specific changes will highlight the various kinds of reform efforts.[9]

Contributing to high attrition and low conviction rates, significant obstacles in the prosecution of rape cases were corroboration requirements, resistance and consent standards, and the admissability of victim reputation evidence. A number of states, such as Michigan, New Mexico and Florida, have repealed corroboration requirements. Traditionally, a rape defendant could not be convicted on the sole basis of victim testimony: Requiring additional evidence or witness statements is related to stereotypes of frequent false reports and victim consent. One dimension of the new rape laws is the removal of this unique feature of rape statutes, making prosecution and conviction more tenable as an outcome.

The redefinition of rape as a graduated series of offenses is a second aspect of reform. Objective criteria upon which to judge the existence as well as the severity of the sexual assault are specified. Reliance on utmost resistance for duration of the attack is removed as the standard for non-consent. Several stages, e.g., Michigan, Minnesota and Ohio, have abolished their resistance requirements in favor of the more objective criteria of absence/presence of force or threat thereof. The specification of objective criteria additionally addresses the problems traditionally surrounding consent: If certain elements are present, e.g., force, injury or weapons, regardless of victim resistance a crime is deemed to have occurred.[10]

A third feature of reform legislation concerns evidence about the victim's past sexual activity. As of 1980, 40 states have limited the admissibility of character/reputation evidence in the courtroom.[11] Most states now "simply require a pre-trial hearing on relevance before evidence regarding the victim's sex conduct with persons other than the defendant can be admitted."[12] A few other states, such as Michigan, have placed rigid limitations on the admissibility of such evidence, essentially admitting evidence only to show the origin of semen, disease or pregnancy.[13]

Other types of reform over the past decade redefine rape as sexual assault, criminal sexual conduct, or sexual battery, and include a wider range of victims (e.g., males, spouses), and a wider range of behaviors in sexual assault statutes (e.g., oral and anal conduct and forced sexual contact, in addition to penetration). Given the different types of legislative changes aimed at abating the discriminatory treatment of rape victims, one might expect a significant decrease in attrition and acquittal rates associated with this offense. This paper will examine the success of these legislative solutions by investigating the attrition or loss of cases before, during and after trial.

MICHIGAN'S MODEL REFORM LAW

In 1974 the state of Michigan passed reform legislation addressing many of the problems with rape prosecution. Michigan's comprehensive statute, the Criminal Sexual Conduct Code, has been referred to as model rape legislation.[14] This code attempted to abolish the de facto corroboration requirement by specifying the lack of its de jure existence. This was accomplished by stating that "the testimony of a victim need not be corroborated in prosecutions."[15] The code eliminates the resistance requirement, stipulating that "a victim need not resist the actor."[16] Instead of using the word consent, the code established criminal sexual conduct in the first, second, third and fourth degrees. These offenses are graduated along objective criteria, such as the absence/presence of weapons, aiders and abettors, and victim injury.[17] The Michigan statute further employed sex-neutral terminology and covered a wide range of sexual acts. The code additionally permitted reputation/character evidence only:

> (1) to the extent that the judge finds that the following proposed evidence is material to a fact at issue in the case and that its inflammatory or prejudicial nature does not outweigh its probative value:
> a. Evidence of the victim's past sexual conduct with the actor.
> b. Evidence of specific instances of sexual activity showing the source of origin of semen, pregnancy or disease.[18]

The Study

One measure of the success of model legislation will be found in attrition and conviction rates. Because the code reformed the major elements contributing to case mortality, the new code might be expected to bring about low attrition and high conviction rates. Not only is the shift in scrutiny meant to lessen victim trauma, but also the encouragement of higher conviction rates is designed to rectify the inequitable treatment of rape. High conviction or low attrition and acquittal rates would be one indicator of implementation meeting the law's objectives.

This study assesses Michigan's legislative act of 1974 by examining attrition and conviction. The implementation of statutory enactments renders legislation successful in impact. Sexual assault prosecutions were scrutinized for a three year period subsequent to the 1974 enactment in order to examine the impact of the model law.

Prosecutorial decision making was singled out in this investigation for two reasons: first, prosecutors are traditionally neglected in the theoretical and research literature. This least studied official is said nonetheless to be the most powerful agent in the administration of justice.[19] Second, the prosecutor alone "activates the judicial machinery,"[20] determines whether to charge, which charges to levy, and whether to plea bargain and nolle cases. The discretionary powers exercised by prosecutors have tremendous impact on rape case treatment. The prosecutor plays a critical role in shaping outcomes.

In examining prosecutorial discretion, the attempt was to discern the types of decisions rendered in sexual assault cases, as well as to specify the stages and extent of attrition. Attrition refers to where and how often charges do not proceed through complete adjudication. The data for this study include all criminal sexual conduct cases in Kalamazoo County, Michigan, between 1975 to 1977, beginning with the first full year of implementation of the 1974 code and continuing through the next two years of operation. Kalamazoo County is a medium sized, relatively urban area, with a population of approximately one/quarter million inhabitants. Data were made available for this project by the county's prosecuting attorney. The attrition rates calculated in this study are discussed, then compared to comparable data in the few similar studies. These comparisons shed light on the use of rape reform law as a means to combat problems such as attrition in rape prosecutions.

APPLICATION AND RESULTS OF THE 1974 MICHIGAN RAPE LAW

Two primary types of attrition rates are pertinent to this investigation. One concerns prosecution, the other convictions. At the first stage of prosecution, cases may drop out of the system after police make an arrest decision. In Kalamazoo, as in most other jurisdictions, police must seek prosecutorial approval by submitting an arrest warrant request before or after a crime suspect is arrested. At this point, prosecutors decide their "causes, cases and targets for prosecution,"[21] either denying or authorizing warrant requests. Warrant denial by prosecutors means that the suspect cannot be picked up/arrested, or if the arrest has already been effected, the suspect must be released because prosecution of the case has been declined. Warrant authorization means that the case will proceed through the criminal justice system. The *prosecution rate* in this study was calculated to reflect the proportion of authorizations given all police requests. The *non-prosecution rate* indicates the percentage of warrant denials given all requests, or the attrition of cases at the charging stage of prosecution.

Once cases are accepted for prosecution they do not automatically terminate with conviction. The *acquittal rate*, reflects the loss of cases due to acquittal/dismissal by juries and judges, or to nolles by prosecutors. One acquittal rate was calculated for authorized cases only, and another for all sexual assault cases based on all warrant requests.

The nonprosecution and acquittal rates comprise the focus of this study, but several other rates were calculated for interpretative purposes. A *conviction rate* indicates the percentage of cases which terminated in guilty verdicts or guilty pleas. One conviction rate was calculated based on all authorized cases—i.e., the proportion of accepted cases which ended in a finding/pleading of guilt—and another on all criminal sexual conduct cases which came to the prosecutor's attention through warrant requests. The latter indicates the overall prosecution and conviction ratio of sexual assault cases.

Finally, the *plea bargaining rate* reflects the percentage of cases involving plea negotiations. Ascertaining guilty pleas assures convictions, which enhance the conviction rates when determined on an overall or an authorized case basis.

The most direct means to assess the effectiveness of Michigan's law would entail a comparison of attrition and acquittal rates before and after the 1974 Code was implemented. Such data were available only for Detroit, and only for the conviction rate based on accepted/authorized cases. Data on warrant requests and authorization/denial were not available for the pre-1974 period in Kalamazoo or any other state jurisdiction. The Detroit data are therefore drawn on for authorized-case comparisons, but are not amenable to interpretations concerning the charging stage of prosecution. Data for the calculation of prosecution rates were available only in the few prosecution studies conducted in other cities in other states. The Michigan law's impact on attrition at the charging stage can be assessed by comparing the prosecution rate in a jurisdiction such as Kalamazoo, operating under model legislation, to prosecution rates in jurisdictions operating under traditional rape statutes.

The acquittal rate—nonconviction of accepted or all cases—can also be compared for the model and traditional legislation jurisdictions. Michigan's law should have led to less attrition/more conviction of attackers if implementation led to a positive impact. This would be reflected in a lower (nonprosecution and) acquittal rate in the Kalamazoo and Detroit data as contrasted to other jurisdictions where such reform laws had not been enacted.

Site Findings

The Kalamazoo data offer some insight into the effectiveness of the law once implemented. Table I summarizes the various rates for Kalamazoo County.

The findings in Kalamazoo County show that prosecutors authorized police-requested charges 46% of the time, while they denied requests or dropped cases at intake in over one/half (54%) the cases. The acquittal rate for authorized cases was 22%, indicating that

TABLE I: ATTRITION AND NON-CONVICTION IN
CRIMINAL SEXUAL CONDUCT CASES, KALAMAZOO, MICHIGAN

Rate	1975-77
Prosecution Rate (authorized/requested warrants)	46%
Non-Prosecution Rate (denials/requested warrants)	54%
Acquittal Rate for Authorized Cases (acquittal, dismissal, and nolle/authorized warrants)	22%
Plea Bargaining Rate (plea bargains/authorized warrants)	58%
Conviction Rate for Authorized Cases (guilty pleas and verdicts/authorized warrants)	73%
Overall Conviction Rate (guilty pleas and verdicts/requested warrants)	34%
Overall Non-Conviction Rate (warrant denials, acquittals, dismissals, and nolles/requested warrants)	64%*

*The overall conviction and attrition rates add to 98 rather than 100% due to missing data.

almost one/quarter of all cases accepted for prosecution were either acquitted/dismissed by judges or juries or nolled by prosecutors. Another way to look at these authorized cases is to examine the conviction rate. Almost three/quarters (73%) of the cases accepted at intake by prosecutors resulted in convictions, either through guilty verdicts or guilty pleas. Over half (58%) of these convictions in the authorized cases were the result of plea negotiations as opposed to trial.

Examination of overall nonconviction rates, those based on all police requested cases rather than on cases accepted by prosecutors, shows that approximately two/thirds (64%) of all criminal sexual conduct cases dropped out at some point in the criminal justice process. This means that prosecutors were able to accept and successfully complete about one/third (34%) of all sexual assaults that came within the purview of their office over the first three years of the new law's operation.

While additional types of data are required to understand the implications of these findings, several preliminary comments about the Michigan Criminal Sexual Code and its implementation can be made. Taken at face value, the various rates in Kalamazoo County appear to indicate limited success with the model code in the first three years of its implementation.

Consideration of what happened in the authorized cases points to a measure of success as a result of implementation process. Once prosecutors decided to proceed with cases at the intake charging stage, they followed through on the cases with a degree of efficacy, as demonstrated by the 73% conviction rate. In other words, prosecutors were able to secure guilty verdicts/pleas in almost three/quarters of all accepted criminal sexual conduct cases. The objective of enhancing prosecution, by making convictions more tenable as an outcome, can be viewed as having met with some success.

The finding that 58% of the authorized cases were plea bargained is amenable to two interpretations. On the one hand, because of plea bargaining, prosecutors ensured convictions and simultaneously saved victims the time and trauma of public court and trial. On the other hand, prosecutors reduced the severity of the charges and/or recommended lighter sentences than allowed by the statute as a part of plea negotiations in more than one/half (58%) of all accepted cases.

From a victim advocate point of view, the warrant denials, acquittals and nolle prosequis can be viewed with disfavor. Slightly over one/half of the sexual assault cases police deemed founded and therefore worthy of pursuit were totally rejected by prosecutors. Aside from denying over one/half of the cases at the outset, prosecutors lost almost an additional quarter of accepted cases through acquittals/dismissals by judges and juries or by their own nolles of charges. The fact that almost two/thirds of all cases coming to the prosecutor's attention were lost at some stage clearly indicates that the phenomena of attrition and nonconviction persisted. Because the new law was enacted to address problems of case mortality and low convictions, and to make easier the prosecution of rape, these findings can be interpreted as unfavorable.

Rate Comparisons Within State

Comparison of these rates with other Michigan data provides one basis for decisive, in-depth interpretation. While only Detroit data were available for comparative assessment, these data were available for the pre- and post-reform law years (1973[22] and 1975-1979[23] respectively). Table II presents these Michigan data.

As Table II indicates, during 1973, the year preceding the passage of the Criminal Sexual Conduct Code, only 10% of all reported rapes in Detroit resulted in arrest warrant authorizations. Of these authorized cases slightly over one/half (55%) resulted in conviction. Overall, only 5% of all reported rapes terminated with convictions by guilty pleas/verdicts. Data on plea bargaining as a means employed to sustain these convictions were unavailable for this pre-1974 period in Detroit.

The only available data for Detroit relevant to rates after the model code was enacted concern nonconviction and plea bargaining for authorized cases. Data on warrant requests and dispositions for Detroit in the post-1974 period were not available. Between 1975 and 1979 approximately 30% of the criminal sexual conduct cases accepted for prosecution in Detroit did not terminate with guilty pleas or verdicts. Almost three/quarters (70.1% to 73.2%, varying by year) of the accepted cases wound up in convictions. Of these convictions, 77% were obtained through guilty pleas entered by defendants.

The pattern demonstrated in Table II with a measure of consistency is the success of the model code in Michigan in the reduction of attrition and enhancement of conviction. Specifically, the percentage of cases accepted for prosecution appears to have increased

TABLE II: ATTRITION AND NON-CONVICTION IN SEXUAL ASSAULT CASES, KALAMAZOO AND DETROIT, MICHIGAN 1973, 1975-79, 1975-77

	Detroit 1973	Detroit 1975-79	Kalamazoo 1975-77
Prosecution Rate	10%	-	46%
Non-Prosecution Rate	90%	-	54%
Acquittal Rate for Authorized Cases	45%	26.8-29.9%*	22%
Plea Bargaining Rate	-	77%	58%
Conviction Rate for Authorized Cases	55%	70.1-73.2%*	73%
Overall Conviction Rate	5%	-	34%
Overall Non-Conviction Rate	95%	-	64%

*Range of variation given over the time period 1975-79.

after the Criminal Sexual Conduct Code was implemented (10% in 1973 Detroit vs. 46%, 1975-1977, in Kalamazoo).[24] The loss of these accepted cases through findings of nonguilt, dismissals, and nolles additionally decreased, from 45% in 1973 in Detroit to approximately 20% in both Detroit and Kalamazoo after the code was enacted, indicating the reduction of nonconviction.[25] The nonattrition or conviction rates for these authorized cases can similarly be interpreted as a measure of the law's success, because there was almost a 20% increase in convictions once prosecutors had accepted cases (the change from a 55% conviction rate in 1973 in Detroit to a 70.1%-73.2% conviction rate between 1975-1979, with Kalamazoo's post model code conviction rate directly paralleling the Detroit experience).[26]

The similarity of authorized case acquittal and conviction rates in Kalamazoo and Detroit indicates that the 1973 Detroit figure of 95% overall nonconviction of rape cases dropped after enactment of the Criminal Sexual Conduct Code, i.e., that the law had a favorable impact on overall case mortality and convictions. The 64% loss of cases overall in Kalamazoo in the post-1974 period compares favorably to the 95% figure. Between 1975-1977, the overall nonattrition or conviction rate of one/third (34%) of all requested cases in Kalamazoo similarly indicates an improvement over the 1973 Detroit figure of 5%.

Data were not available on plea bargaining in Michigan for the time preceding the model code. After the law's enactment, however, both the Detroit and Kalamazoo jurisdictions plea bargained over one/half of their sexual assault cases, with figures of 77% and 58% respectively. The new law at least facilitated the use of plea bargaining, a process which enhanced convictions in both locations.

Comparisons with Traditional Law Jurisdictions

The effectiveness of the Michigan Criminal Sexual Conduct Code in abating attrition and low convictions in sexual assault prosecutions can be further assessed through comparative data from other communities.[27] There were two research projects which presented relevant data. The first study to provide data on attrition in rape was conducted in Washington, D.C.[28] The second covered Kansas City, Missouri and Seattle, Washington.[29]

The kind of rape legislation existing in these locations differed. Washington, D.C., has a traditional rape statute which dichotomizes rape into forcible and statutory offenses and stipulates that the crime involves carnal knowledge of a female, forcibly and against her will.[30] Although minor alterations were enacted in the 1970s,[31] Kansas City, Missouri, also has an essentially traditional rape law. Seattle, Washington, incorporates some reform measures, but not the type of model legislation enacted in Michigan.[32]

Table III shows the attrition for the different jurisdictions. As can be seen, the prosecution rates vary from a low of one/fourth to a high of almost three/fourths of all cases charged by prosecutors. The rank order of the prosecution rates most favorable to a victim advocate would be Washington, D.C. (70%), Kalamazoo (46%), and Kansas City/Seattle (25%). Given the different codes operating in these jurisdictions, this result is not the expected one. The model legislation jurisdiction (Kalamazoo) would presumably have had the highest prosecution rate, because the law was designed to encourage prosecution.

To understand the implications of this finding it is necessary to examine the other attrition and nonconviction rates. Scrutiny of ad-

TABLE III. ATTRITION AND NON-CONVICTION IN SEXUAL ASSAULT CASES
KALAMAZOO, WASHINGTON, D.C., AND KANSAS CITY/SEATTLE

	Kalamazoo (1975-77)	Washington, D.C. (1973)	Kansas City/ Seattle (1978)
Prosecution Rate	46%	70%	25%
Non-Prosecution Rate	54%	30%	75%
Acquittal Rate for Authorized Cases	22%	65%	27%
Plea Bargaining Rate	58%	22%	-
Convicted Rate for Authorized Cases	73%	33%	45%
Overall Conviction Rate	34%	23%	14%
Overall Non-Conviction Rate	64%	76%	86%

ditional rates indicates that not only is it misleading to examine the prosecution rate alone, but further that a very different summary interpretation, such as a ranking of favorable rates by city, can be reached.

The misleading nature of judging success by nonattrition at only one stage of prosecution becomes evident when attention is directed to the overall conviction and nonconviction rates. The overall nonconviction rate was lowest in Kalamazoo and highest in Kansas City/Seattle. Similarly, the highest overall conviction rate pertained to the Kalamazoo jurisdiction and the lowest to Kansas City/Seattle. Given the model legislation it would be anticipated that the Kalamazoo jurisdiction would experience the least attrition. Moreover, this pattern denotes a realization of the objective to minimize case losses. Further inquiry needs to be made, because the Washington, D.C., data might have been expected to exhibit the worst rather than middle ground figures on attrition. Traditional legislation operates in the District of Columbia jurisdiction, as compared to the basically traditional but slightly mixed laws in Kansas City and Seattle.

An explanation for the figures in Washington, D.C., relative to those for Kansas City and Seattle, can be found by re-examining the prosecution rates. The Washington, D.C., figures on overall conviction and nonconviction were better than Kansas City and Seattle figures, because prosecutors authorized such a high percentage of cases at the initial in-take screening stage. Washington, D.C., experienced the least attrition early on in the criminal justice process, yielding a more favorable overall conviction rate than Kansas City and Seattle.[33]

Authorizing a high percentage of cases does not necessarily result in optimal net gains such as high conviction rates. The evidence for this proposition is derived from the Washington, D.C., results where the highest prosecution rate did not yield the highest conviction or the lowest acquittal rates. What happens to cases after the charges have been levied by prosecutors? Two/thirds (65%) of the cases accepted for prosecution in Washington, D.C., did not result in findings or pleadings of guilt, contributing to a relatively high overall nonconviction or low conviction rate. The lowest acquittal and nonconviction rates were associated with the Kalamazoo jurisdiction, which authorized approximately one/half (45%) as opposed to over two/thirds (70%) of the sexual assault cases.

Plea bargaining presents an important consideration in relation to these rates. The Kalamazoo data displayed both the highest conviction (73%) and plea bargaining (58%) rates. The frequent use of plea bargaining in Kalamazoo is directly related to the large proportion of convictions for authorized cases. It can be argued that the success evident in the Kalamazoo rates is partly due to the model legislation. Flexibility in plea bargaining is enhanced by the Criminal Sexual Conduct Code which permits four degrees of sexual assault as opposed to strictly forcible and statutory rape categories. The model code allows prosecutors greater discretionary latitude in plea negotiations because of the wider variety of charges on which guilty pleas can be accepted, and because of the broad range of sentences and thus sentence recommendations possible.[34] These may be offered in exchange for guilty pleas. This increased flexibility in plea bargaining facilitates guilty pleas and hence convictions. The Detroit data showing a 77% plea bargaining rate and approximately 70% conviction rate for accepted cases (Table II) supports this interpretation.

Higher plea bargaining rates are not necessarily desirable from a victim advocate point of view. When plea bargaining rates are low, yielding a lower conviction rate (as in the Washington D.C., study), a gain may, in fact, be made in terms of more severe sentencing for those cases that result in guilt at trial. This sort of trade-off should be borne in mind when discussing attrition.

In terms of acquittal and conviction rates, the Michigan jurisdictions fared most favorably. Both jurisdictions operating under model legislation had the lowest acquittal and highest conviction rates. The implementation of the code appears to have met with some measure of success by rendering sexual assault case prosecution and conviction more feasible than before the legislation's enactment.

Nonetheless, attrition and nonconviction in sexual assault cases remain a problem. Even in the Michigan jurisdictions, acquittal was the outcome in roughly one/quarter of accepted cases (22% Kalamazoo, 26.8%-29.9% Detroit). And, because over one/half of the cases never get beyond the warrant authorization stage (54% Kalamazoo), almost two/thirds (64% Kalamazoo) of all cases brought to prosecutors suffered.

While the law may be radically altered, requirements and practices for prosecuting rape suspects remain problematic. Prosecutors may not (be able to) authorize criminal sexual conduct cases because the cases are too weak to take to trial or even too weak to have any leverage for plea bargaining. The Criminal Sexual Conduct Codes stipulates criteria for the various degrees; but many cases the police believe founded apparently do not meet the standard necessary for prosecution, if the prosecution rate, even under the new code, is an indication. Lack of evidence such as injuries in addition to the sexual assault, or weak evidence such as a small number of witnesses, influence prosecutors' charging and plea bargaining decisions in criminal sexual conduct cases.[35]

It is tenable that the persisting de facto need for more evidence, etc., is due to a lack of change in prosecutorial attitudes. It is also tenable that prosecutors, as the victim's representative, have aligned themselves with the attitude change as manifest in reform statutes, yet are thwarted in practice. If their views have changed, their anticipations about judicial/juror attitudes may preclude authorizations and/or necessitate plea bargains for lesser charges and/or sentences.[36]

Regardless of the explanation entertained, a conclusion of success is questionable. Despite the findings that the two model code cities compared favorably to the traditional law jurisdictions, these cities still experienced attrition, as evidenced by the acquittal and overall nonconviction rates.

CONCLUSIONS

In examining whether the model rape reform statute was effective in Kalamazoo County, attrition and lack of convictions were found to be continuing problems with the prosecution of criminal sexual conduct cases. The findings indicated an overall loss of 64% of the cases which came to the attention of the prosecutor. Approximately one half of the cases were denied for prosecution at intake and 58% were plea bargained to lesser charges or for lesser sentences than allowed by the Criminal Sexual Conduct statute. Of those cases accepted, 22% resulted in judicial acquittal or prosecutor nolles.

Comparison of the Kalamazoo data to pre-reform rates from Detroit suggested that the law was effective in reducing the magnitude of these problems. Further comparisons of the two Michigan jurisdiction rates after reform to three basically traditional rape law jurisdictions (Washington, D.C., and Kansas City/Seattle) strengthened the viability of such an interpretation. A measure of success in the implementation of the model code was evident in lower attrition of cases. In addition, the removal of unique and discriminatory requirements and standards in the 1974 Michigan statute can be seen as effective, because higher conviction rates were achievable. The degree structure of sexual assault offenses in Michigan is also beneficial, not only because it covers a broad range of criminal behaviors, but also because it facilitates plea bargaining.

Several additional considerations require elaboration. The use of plea bargaining in sexual assault cases may advantageously sustain convictions, but may also have deleterious effects. Two frequent types of plea negotiation agreements are prosecutorial recommendations for relatively lenient sentencing by judges and agreements to permit the accused to plead guilty to a lesser related offense—by definition carrying lesser penalties—in exchange for the guilty plea. Rapists who are convicted by plea bargained guilty pleas serve shorter sentences than those convicted at trial. Sexual assault victims, thus, see the men who raped them receive light(er) penalties and obtain release from institutions in short(er) amounts of time than those adjudicated guilty at trial. The trade-off between high conviction rates and more lenient sentences (even ranging to probation) must be considered in the evaluation of differential rates of prosecution. Future research might productively examine the relationship between trial and plea bargaining dispositions and sentencing outcomes with the use of sentencing data.

That legislation alone can abate the double burden for rape victims is doubtful. It is asserted here that while attempts at reform legislation represent a step in the right direction, alone they seem to fall short of meeting stated goals. Even positively altered legislation has pitfalls, as evidenced in this paper. For example, a 64% rate of overall nonconviction was found to exist in Kalamazoo, Michigan, even after model legislation was implemented. Further evidence that legislative reform represents insufficient change can be found in the de facto corroboration requirements in most jurisdictions throughout the country, despite the nonexistence or removal of de jure requirements.[37] Michigan sought to eliminate this de facto requirement by specifying its lack of de jure standing; whether this legislative solution was successful remains to be seen.[38]

Implementation of legislation cannot be assumed to mirror legislative objectives.[39] The passage of legislation should be viewed as only a first measure. Laws as well as the beliefs, perceived vested interests, and power structure must all be addressed jointly if real change is to come about. If myths are not dispelled, and attitudes about sexual assault and its victims are not changed, they will likely permeate the implementation of even model legislation and operate to preclude the amelioration of problems attending the prosecution of this crime. The alteration of legal codes by itself seems to be only partially successful. Misguided, erroneous beliefs and historically grounded discriminatory tactics must be replaced with new awareness, realistic attitudes and humane practices.

ENDNOTES

1. See for example Carol Bohmer and Audrey Blumberg, "Twice Traumatized: The Rape Victim and the Court," 58 *Judicature* 341 (1975); Susan Brownmiller, *Against Our Will: Men, Women and Rape* (New York: Simon & Schuster, 1975); Lynda Lytle Holmstrom and Ann Wolbert Burgess, "Rape: The Victim Goes on Trial," in *Victimology: A New Focus*, ed. Israel Drapkin and Emilio Viano (Lexington, Massachusetts: D. C. Heath, 1975); David Luginbill, "Repeal of the Corroboration Requirement: Will It Tip the Scales of Justice?" 24 *Drake Law Review* 669 (1975); Helene Sasko and Deborah Sesek, "Rape Reform Legislation: Is It the Solution?" 24 *Cleveland State Law Review* 463 (1975); Julia R. and Herman Schwendinger, *Rape and Inequality* (Beverly Hills: Sage, 1983).

2. Camile E. LeGrand, "Rape and Rape Laws: Sexism in Society and the Law," 61 *California Law Review* 919 (1973); Gerald D. Robin, "Forcible Rape: Institutionalized Sexism in the Criminal Justice System," 26 *Crime and Delinquency* 136 (1977); Martin D. Schwartz and Todd R. Clear, "Toward a New Law on Rape," 26 *Crime and Delinquency* 129 (1980); Julia and Herman Schwendinger, *Rape and Inequality*, pp. 170-31.

3. Federal Bureau of Investigation, *Uniform Crime Reports: Crime in the United States* (Washington, D.C.: U.S. Government Printing Office, 1973), p. 15; U.S., Department of

Justice, Bureau of Justice Statistics, *Criminal Victimization in the United States* (Washington, D.C.: U.S. Government Printing Office, 1979), p. 15; Susan Brownmiller, *Against Our Will*, p. 190; Lynn A. Curtis, "Present and Future Measures of Victimization in Forcible Rape," in *Sexual Assault: The Victim and the Rapist*, ed. Marcia J. Walker and Stanley Brodsky (Lexington, Massachusetts: Lexington Books, 1979), pp. 61-68.

4. Federal Bureau of Investigation, *Uniform Crime Reports* (Washington, D.C.: U.S. Government Printing Office, 1979), p. 15.

5. Federal Bureau of Investigation, *Uniform Crime Reports* (Washington, D.C.: U.S. Government Printing Office, 1980), p. 178.

6. Federal Bureau of Investigation, *Uniform Crime Reports* (Washington, D.C.: U.S. Government Printing Office, 1975), p. 24.

7. National Institute of Law Enforcement and Criminal Justice, Law Enforcement Assistance Administration, *Forcible Rape: Final Project Report* (Washington, D.C.: U.S. Government Printing Office, March 1978), pp. ix, 57.

8. Herbert S. Field and Leigh B. Bienen, *Jurors and Rape: A Study in Psychology and Law* (Lexington, Massachusetts: Lexington Books, 1980), p. 153.

9. See *ibid.* for an inventory of state statutes and changes.

10. See for example *The Michigan Criminal Sexual Conduct Code*, P.A. 226 (1974).

11. Herbert Field and Leigh Bienen, *Jurors and Rape*, p. 171.

12. *Ibid.*

13. P.A. 226, Section 520(j).

14. Jan BenDor, "Justice After Rape: Legal Reform in Michigan," in *Sexual Assault*, ed. Marcia Walker and Stanley Brodsky, pp. 149-60; Charles W. Dean and Mary deBruyn-Kops, *The Crime and Consequences of Rape* (Springfield, Illinois: Charles C. Thomas, 1982); Herbert Field and Leigh Bienen, *Jurors and Rape*; National Institute of Law Enforcement and Criminal Justice, *Forcible Rape*.

15. P.A. 266, Section 520(h).

16. *Ibid.*, Section 520(i).

17. *Ibid.*, Sections 520(b)(c).

18. *Ibid.*, Section 520(j).

19. George Cole, *The American System of Criminal Justice* (North Sciturate, Massachusetts: Duxbery Press, 1975); Abraham S. Blumberg, *Criminal Justice: Issues and Ironies* (New York: New Viewpoints, 1979), p. 227.

20. Delmar Karlen and T. Laurence Schultz, "Justice in the Accusation," in *The Rights of the Accused: In Law and Action*, ed. Stuart S. Nagel (Beverly Hills, California: Sage Publications, 1975), p. 13.

21. Abraham Blumberg, *Criminal Justice*, p. 123.

22. Jan BenDor, "Justice After Rape," in *Sexual Assault: The Victim and the Rapist*, ed. Marcia Walker and Stanley Brodsky.

23. Jeanne C. Marsh, Alison Geist and Nathan Caplan, *Rape and the Limits of Law Reform* (Boston: Auburn House Publishing Company, 1982).

24. The difference in the prosecution rate of Detroit in the pre- and Kalamazoo in the post-Criminal Sexual Conduct Code periods is not a direct measure of change because of the different research sites; it may, however, be taken as indicative of success with the model code. As the problem of attrition before rape reform statutes was pervasive nation-wide, there is no reason to suspect that Kalamazoo's pre-1974 prosecution rate was higher than Detroit's.

25. This comparison is based on the same logic described above. Support of this reasoning is additionally found in the similarity between Detroit and Kalamazoo data over a period of years subsequent to the reform legislation (1975-1979 Detroit, 1975-1977 Kalamazoo).

26. The pre- and post-conviction rates reported for Michigan in Jeanne Marsh, Alison Geist and Nathan Caplan, *Rape and the Limits of Law Reform*, are consistent with these data and this interpretations.

27. Because data on prosecutors' charging decisions are unavailable for other Michigan jurisdictions, and because they are little available on plea bargaining and convictions in

Michigan and elsewhere, it must be cautioned that generalizations to Michigan or to national patterns, based upon the data and discussion in this paper, would be unwarranted. The findings and comparisons described herein are instructive for heuristic purposes in pointing to implications for legal reform and sexual assault prosecutions.

28. Kristen M. Williams, *The Prosecution of Sexual Assault* (Washington, D.C.: Institute for Law and Policy Research, 1978), pp. 23-28.

29. National Institute of Law Enforcement and Criminal Justice, *Forcible Rape*, p. 49.

30. See Herbert Field and Leigh Bienen, *Jurors and Rape*, for state statistics.

31. *Ibid.*

32. *Ibid.* Unfortunately the data from Kansas City and Seattle were not provided separately. One state has traditional legislation and the other, minor types of reform. Because of the need to interpret findings in an aggregate manner, the jurisdictions studied by the National Institute of Law enforcement of Criminal Justice will be treated as having essentially traditional legislation.

33. It should be noted that Washington, D.C., has a well organized anti-rape group which may help to account for the high prosecution rate despite the traditional rape legislation operating in this jurisdiction.

34. P.A. 266.

35. Susan Caringella-MacDonald, "Factors Influencing Prosecutorial Discretion in Criminal Sexual Conduct Cases," paper presented to annual meeting of the American Psychological Association, Montreal, 1980.

36. The results of interview data reported in Jeanne Marsh, Alison Geist and Nathan Caplan, *Rape and the Limits of Legal Reform*, support the latter interpretation, that criminal justice officials' attitudes have not kept pace with legal change.

37. Richard A. Hibey, "The Trial of a Rape Case: An Advocate's Analysis of Corroboration, Consent, and Character," in *Rape Victimology*, ed. Leroy Schultz (Springfield: Charles C. Thomas, 1975); Note, "The Rape Corroboration Requirement: Repeal Not Reform," 81 *Yale Law Journal* 1365 (1975); H.S. Shapo, "Recent Statutory Developments in the Definition of Forcible Rape," 61 *Virginia Law Review* 1500 (1975).

38. The author has research of this nature presently underway.

39. See for example Piers Bierne and Richard Quinney, ed., *Marxism and Law* (New York: Wiley, 1982); W.G. Carson, "The Sociology of Crime and the Emergence of Criminal Laws," in *Deviance and Social Control*, ed. Paul Rock and Mary McIntosh (London: Tavistock Publications, 1974); David Greenberg, ed., *Crime and Capitalism: Readings in Marxist Criminology* (Palo Alto, California: Mayfield Publishing, 1981); Richard Quinney, *Class, State and Crime* (New York: Longman, 1980).

PART III: PROSTITUTION

The reality is that men and women are both participants in prostitution. Laws and enforcement have traditionally been directed only against the women. Contributors to this section examine the contrast between legislative intent and practical implementation of prostitution laws at the local and federal levels.

Marlene Beckman examines the federal anti-prostitution legislation, the Mann Act, in the years following its enactment. She finds that despite congressional intent to punish only procurors, the female victims were punished and sent to prison.

Frances Bernat evaluates the impact of the revised 1978 New York State prostitution law in Buffalo, New York. The new law makes prostitution a sex neutral crime and upgrades the patron offense from a violation to a misdemeanor. Despite these legal changes, Bernat finds that Buffalo police practices have not altered and that women, far more often than men, continue to be arrested. Both Bernat and Beckman show that at the local and national level, legislative intent was thwarted at the implementation stage.

The White Slave Traffic Act: Historical Impact of a Federal Crime Policy on Women

Marlene D. Beckman

ABSTRACT. When Congress passed the White Slave Traffic Act, legislators were strongly influenced by early twentieth century progressive era reformers, who sought to rid the country of commercial prostitution. The statute was directed at the elimination of the business of securing women and girls and selling them outright or exploiting them for immoral purposes. Instead, it was used to prosecute the voluntary and ordinary immoralities of people and to punish the women "victims" whom the law was designed to protect.

On June 25, 1910, Congress passed the White Slave Traffic Act, known as the Mann Act. Progressive era reformers used the catchwords "white slavery" to promote the vision of women held in bondage against their will, of mysterious druggings and abductions of helpless young girls, and of unexplained disappearances of innocent and naive immigrants forced into lives of prostitution and vice. Yet, just several years later, law enforcement officials relied on the White Slave Traffic Act to arrest, prosecute and send to prison a man and a woman who traveled from Jersey City to spend the weekend in New York.

This paper will show how the White Slave Traffic Act was misapplied. The Mann Act was to be directed at the elimination of the business of securing women and girls and selling them outright or exploiting them for immoral purposes. Instead, it was used to prose-

---

Marlene D. Beckman, U.S. Department of Justice, Washington, D.C. I acknowledge Dr. Claudine SchWeber, Criminal Justice Department, State University College at Buffalo, for getting me started and Wendy Williams, Georgetown University Law Center, for keeping me going.

cute the voluntary and ordinary immoralities of people and to punish the women "victims" whom the law was designed to protect.

DEVELOPMENT AND EXPANSION OF THE WHITE SLAVE TRAFFIC ACT

The White Slave Traffic Act made it a federal crime to engage in prostitution in interstate commerce. The act provided heavy penalties for transporting or in any way aiding, abetting or causing the transporting in interstate or foreign commerce of "any woman or girl for the purpose of prostitution or debauchery, or for any other immoral purpose."[1]

In more than one sense, the name "White Slave Traffic Act" remains a misnomer.[2] First, the act makes no distinction as to the race or the color of the female whose transportation is a violation of the law. Second, in many instances the "victims" willingly consented to the practices in which they were engaged. Nonetheless, Congress gave the act its name because the central purpose of it was to halt what many believed was a serious and widespread practice: foreign-born commercial procurers taking innocent young girls and women by force and holding them captive with threats to their lives, a practice held to resemble black servitude in its exploitative and barbarous nature.

The legislators were influenced by what was taking place in the country. In no period of U.S. history did the custodians of morality direct more serious attention to the eradication of prostitution than during the first two decades of the twentieth century known as the progressive era.[3] The energetic outburst against white slave traffic grew out of the progressive's view that women were naturally chaste and virtuous, and no woman became a whore unless she had first been raped, seduced, drugged or deserted. The image of the prostitute, developed by reformers, was of a lonely and confused female. In the search for explanations of what could have led girls so to degrade and ultimately destroy themselves, the progressive formula maintained that female prostitutes were passive victims of social disequilibrium and the brutality of men. This conception of female weakness and male domination left no room for the possibility that prostitutes might consciously or aggressively choose their activities.[4]

A review of the historical development of the Mann Act reveals two themes. First, Congress intended the act to apply only to commercial vice and those cases where there was evidence of coercion.[5] Second, the act was not intended to apply to ordinary prostitution, control of which remained within the police powers of the states.[6] Instead, Congress intended to supplement local authority by reaching interstate transportation for commercial purposes. Despite this clear congressional intent, inclusion in the statute of the words "any other immoral purpose" had an unforeseen effect: the prosecution of non-commercial sex as a federal crime.

In the 1917 case, *Caminetti* v. *United States*, the U.S. Supreme Court first upheld convictions under the act where there was no evidence that the women were prostitutes, that their actions were involuntary, or that the defendants derived any profit except their own pleasure. In *Caminetti* two men voluntarily accompanied by two women traveled from California to Reno, Nevada, for the weekend. The five-justice majority, relying on the plain meaning of the words "any other immoral purpose," upheld the convictions on the grounds the Mann Act applied to voluntary acts of immorality, even when no commercial intention or business profit was shown.[7]

While opportunities to overrule *Caminetti* subsequently presented themselves, the Court continued to rely on this landmark case. In 1946 it reaffirmed the *Caminetti* holding in *Cleveland* v. *United States* by finding that "other immoral purposes" applied to a Morman who, in practicing polygamy, had frequently transported his wives across state lines.[8] Cases such as *Cleveland* show that the clause "any other immoral purpose" was so broad, it could be used to reach any conduct that fell within the popular understanding of immorality. For a time, the federal courts relied on the controversial immoral status concept to become a censor of the nation's sexual morals. The term "other immoral acts" was held to apply to the interstate transportaton of a woman to work as a chorus girl in a theatre where the woman was exposed to smoking, drinking and cursing;[9] a dentist who met his young lover in a neighboring state and shared a hotel room to discuss her pregnancy;[10] two students at the University of Puerto Rico who had sexual intercourse on the way home from a date;[11] and a man and woman who lived together for four years and traveled around the country as man and wife while the man sold securities.[12]

The activity prohibited by the Mann Act was transportation of "any woman or girl" in interstate commerce. On a plain reading of the act, Congress intended the woman who was to engage in sexual conduct to be treated as the person "transported" and the persons who accompanied her or assisted in her transportation were to be prosecuted as "transporters." Only the latter were targeted by the act's criminal sanctions. The courts, however, went beyond the law's objectives.

While two early cases established that a woman could not be an "accomplice" to the offense of transporting herself from one state to another for immoral purposes, the Court held that the woman may be indicted for *conspiracy*.[13] A woman could have conspired to "commit an offense against the United States" within the meaning of the federal statute, although the objective of the conspiracy was her own transportation in interstate commerce for the purpose of prostitution. The extension of the law of conspiracy to include the woman would, the Court reasoned in the 1915 case of *United States v. Holte*, prevent victimization of men. The spectre of blackmail, whereby a woman would lure a man to cross a state line with her and then, by threatening to notify authorities, extort money from him, moved the Court to find a way to prosecute the woman, the language of the act notwithstanding. The woman could now be punished for blackmail or for malicious prosecution. Justice Holmes, writing for the majority in *Holte*, made clear the Court's position:

> We think that it would be going too far to say that the defendant could not be guilty in this case. Suppose, for instance, that a professional prostitute, as well able to look out for herself as was the man, should suggest and carry out a journey within the Act of 1910 in the hope of blackmailing the man, and should buy the railroad tickets, or should pay the fare from Jersey City to New York, she would be within the letter of the Act of 1910, and we see no reason why the act should not be held to apply. We see equally little reason for not treating the preliminary agreement as a conspiracy that the law can reach, if we *abandon the illusion that the woman always is the victim.*[14]

In the 1932 case of *Gebardi v. United States*, the Court looked again at this issue and held that for the woman to fall within the ban of the Mann Act, she must at least aid or assist someone else in transporting or procuring transportation for her, and such aid and assistance must be more active than mere acquiescence.[15] This retreat from the broader implications of the earlier *Holte* decision may be explained on the ground that the *Gebardi* Court was confronted with a woman whose only immoral action was acquiescence to interstate transportation, as opposed to the situation in *Holte* in which the woman was actually a prostitute. The facts of *Gebardi* made the need for establishing limits to the *Holte* principle apparent. In fact, the *Gebardi* Court's conclusion was consistent with the contemporary view that women's criminality was due primarily to their economic and psychological dependence on men. It was also more attuned to the act's original philosophy than was the *Holte* decision.

ENFORCEMENT OF THE MANN ACT

In 1969 William Seagle, a commentator on the Mann Act, asserted that the critics of the Mann Act who had made a "bogey law" out of its sweeping potentialities had failed to consider the selectivity that prosecuting officials exercised in the enforcement of the act. Seagle maintained that although the decisions of the courts had allowed wide latitude to law enforcement authorities, U.S. Attorneys had taken little advantage of this latitude; rather, absent commercial vice, they prosecuted only those cases involving highly aggravated circumstances.[16] The evidence, however, contradicts the Seagle theory. Official circulars issued by the U.S. Department of Justice reveal that the Attorney General, concerned about "federal courts allowing themselves to be turned into ordinary police courts," cautioned prosecutors to use their discretion in noncommercial cases. Nevertheless, my review of the official files of individuals convicted under this law suggests that U.S. Attorneys did not exercise the desired restraint.[17] F.B.I. statistics obtained for this project also confirm the finding.[18]

After *Caminetti* established, in 1917, that commercialism was not an essential element of a Mann Act violation, the Attorney General issued a circular outlining the elements of aggravation required for prosecution in noncommercial cases. The guidelines restricted prosecution in noncommercial cases to "those cases involving a fraudulent overreaching, or involving previously chaste, or very young women or girls, or (when State laws are inadequate) involving married women (with young children) then living with their husbands . . . ." The guidelines further provided "that blackmail cases should, so far as possible, be avoided; and that whenever the women herself voluntarily and without any overreaching, has consented to the criminal arrangement she, too, if the case shall seem to demand it, may be prosecuted as a conspirator." These guidelines represented a significant departure from the congressional intent, articulated in the legislative history, to punish only the procuror or transporter of an unwilling victim of commercial vice.[19]

These instructions were re-issued every year from 1917 to 1932.[20] During the 15-year period, the U.S. Attorneys continued to prosecute individuals engaged in strictly personal sexual escapades that in no way involved either commercial gain or exploitation of innocent victims. The evidence presented here cannot be explained by an occasional error on the part of federal prosecutors in judging the circumstances of a particular case to be "aggravated."

A more likely explanation for this overzealous enforcement was the emergence, at the same time, of the Federal Bureau of Investigation (F.B.I.) as a national police force. As one of the first laws to create a "federal" crime, the Mann Act allowed the new crime-fighting office to prove its mettle. F.B.I. agents were encouraged to present to U.S. Attorneys for a decision on prosecution those complaints which alleged interstate transportation but failed to indicate the existence of prostitution.[21] Further, agents actually filed complaints against victims charging them with conspiracy in order to keep them in custody. If the victim later cooperated, she was not prosecuted on a charge of conspiracy because U.S. Attorneys viewed her as a valuable witness. Arrests of women were thus used to induce them to testify against their male "transporters."[22]

In 1932, one month after the *Gebardi* case was decided, the Attorney General altered the guidelines for prosecution for the first time since *Caminetti*. The Attorney General advised that as a result of the *Gebardi* decision, "a woman, by consenting to go and voluntarily going from one state to another with a man, with a view to immoral relations with him, does not violate the conspiracy statute." He instructed U.S. Attorneys to drop from their list of priorities the prosecution of "the woman herself who voluntarily and without any overreaching has consented to the criminal arrangement."[23] Thus, although before *Gebardi* U.S. Attorneys prosecuted women for conspiracy under the Mann Act whether commercial prostitution was involved, the only cases indicting women after *Gebardi* did involve prostitution, albeit sometimes only on an extremely limited scale. Women engaged in prostitution for a short time in order to earn a few dollars for support could hardly be considered models of the commercial vice that concerned Congress when it passed the Mann Act in 1910.[24]

THE WOMEN IN ALDERSON

After 1927, female violators of the Mann Act were sent to the Federal Industrial Institution for Women in Alderson, West Virginia, which was opened that year as the first and only federal prison exclusively for women. Prior to 1927, female federal prisoners were housed in state correctional facilities. Early records of the women incarcerated for Mann Act violations support the hypothesis that the objectives of the White Slave Traffic Act were thwarted in two ways: 1) by prosecuting individuals who were not involved in commercial vice, but rather engaging in ordinary sexual behavior and 2) by prosecuting the female "victims" of a law designed to "protect" women.

The author examined the records of 156 women committed to Alderson for Mann Act violations between the years 1927 and 1937. This sample represents 87% of the total number of women committed for Mann Act violations during this period.[25] The women were divided into four groups based on the extent of commercial vice associated with their offense.[26]

1. Group one consists of those women with no prostitution or commercial activity of any kind connected with their arrest (n=36, 23%). For the most part, these women were traveling with men across state lines, and either one or both of them was married to someone else. One predominant pattern involved single women traveling with men they loved and hoped to marry, but who turned out to be already married; both the woman and the man were arrested as co-conspirators when the man's wife turned them in.
2. Group two includes those women whose prostitution was incidental to their interstate travels with a man, who was sometimes their husband (n=25, 16%). A common pattern here involved a woman who, at the man's insistence, engaged in isolated instances of prostitution to earn enough money so that they could complete their journey.
3. Group three is composed of women involved in commercial prostitution (n=23, 15%). Typically, such women worked in a brothel or house of ill-repute, and were arrested when they solicited at a hotel, and in so doing crossed the state line. These women had become prostitutes to earn enough money to support themselves.

4. Group four is comprised of women who, themselves often prostitutes, were arrested for aiding or securing transportation for another woman to cross state lines for prostitution (n = 72, 46%). At one extreme was the madame who actually ran the brothel and recruited new workers; at the other was the woman who wrote a letter to a friend back home suggesting that she might do well to come north and join her in her illegal activity. In one case, a woman was sentenced to 18 months because she gave a friend's name to her boyfriend for this purpose. A factor in this indictment may also have been the fact the woman and her boyfriend were, at the time of the arrest, living together as man and wife.

The women in group one were not involved in commercialized vice and further did not fit the profile of the "aggravated" noncommercial cases that had been established by the Attorney General as targets for federal prosecution. On the contrary, most of these cases contain no hint of commercialism nor of the aggravating circumstances required by the prosecution guidelines. Excerpts from the personal history files of two women in group one are illustrative.

Viola had known Blake since she was eight years old—he owned a tin shop and she worked in his office, sending out bills and answering the phone. A friend of his came to the shop by the name of Thomas. He was 24 years old and married, but not living with his wife. Viola became infatuated with Thomas. Her family objected to her working for Blake and she finally left home. Blake told her that he was going to close his shop and go away with Loretta and suggested that she go along with Thomas. Viola agreed and they left Pittsburgh and went as far as Fredericksburg, Virginia where they stayed all night, Loretta and Blake registering as man and wife, and Viola and Thomas as man and wife. The next two days they took turns driving and sleeping. The fourth day they decided to separate: she had had quite enough of the trip and wanted to go home. While the two men were willing to send the girls home, Loretta didn't want to be discarded, so she telephoned the police and reported that they were being beaten. All four were arrested and charged with Mann Act violations.

When Elizabeth was 15, she secured employment as a domestic in order to get away from an unhappy home. There were nine children in all, and as long as Elizabeth stayed at home, she had to wash, iron and cook for her brothers and sisters only to get unkind words in repay for her efforts. Elizabeth left home and went to live with a maternal aunt who sympathized with her. While she was staying with this aunt, she met and fell in love with a man named Steve. He proposed to her but postponed the date of marriage. Steve asked Elizabeth to accompany him on his business trips to deliver liquor. She did and stayed with him at a hotel as his wife. They made 11 trips until they were both arrested on the road in Fairmont, West Virginia. It was then that Elizabeth first learned that Steve was married and that his wife had turned them in.

Overall, the women in group one cannot be described as fitting the profile of aggravated noncommercial cases. Fifteen of the 36 women are under 20 years of age, 14 are in their 20s, and 7 others are in their 30s. The majority, or 25 of the 36 women, had been married at an earlier time. Only 9, however, were married and living with their husbands at the time of their offense; 13 were separated and 3 were divorced. Only 14 had any children at all and, in 2 of those cases, the children were grown and no longer dependents.[27]

This prosecutorial "indiscretion" in noncommercial cases slowed down only after 1932 when the Attorney General directed U.S. Attorneys to drop women as targets in noncommercial cases. As indicated in Figure 1, after *Gebardi*, women were committed in only five noncommercial cases; in three instances the man involved left behind a wife and children; in the fourth case the woman had an illegitimate child with the man; and in the fifth case, the couple were prosecuted for Mann Act violations only after they were apprehended for holding up a gas station. Women in group two—those women to whom prostitution was incidental to their interstate travels—were still being sent to prison but also in smaller numbers. Eighteen of the 25 in this group were convicted before *Gebardi*, while 7 were convicted following *Gebardi*.[28]

Across all 4 groups, the average age is 28 years with the most pronounced age cluster in the 24 to 30 year old bracket. This is a significant departure from the progressive era stereotype of prostitutes as girls whose youthfulness, naivete and inexperience with the world betrayed them. Also, extending across the entire sample, 107 (69%) were not living with a husband; the majority were separated or divorced. Significantly, few of the women had any dependent

TABLE 1a - DESCRIPTION OF MANN ACT VIOLATORS BY *NUMBER* AND GROUP FOR YEARS 1927-1937

Group	Marital Status[1]				Age				Race			Citizenship			Education			IQ[2]			Children[3]			Prior[4] Convictions			Sentence (Yrs)			Region Where[5] Prosecuted		
	S	M	Dv		16-19	20-29	30+		W	Blk		USA	Other		None	8th	9th+		50-75	76+		0	1-2	3+		None	1+		1-19	2-5		South	Midwest	Other
1(N=36)	11	9	16		15	14	7		35	1		36	0		32	4		25	11		22	8	6		33	3		28	8		27	7	2
2(N=25)	7	6	12		5	18	2		25	0		24	1		15	10		13	12		17	7	1		19	6		20	5		19	6	0
3(N=23)	7	7	9		2	19	2		22	1		23	0		16	7		17	6		22	1	0		16	7		18	5		17	3	3
4(N=72)	13	27	32		2	28	42		68	4		67	5		59	13		47	25		42	26	4		38	34		35	37		28	22	22
Total (N=156)	38	49	69		24	79	53		150	6		150	6		122	34		102	54		103	42	11		106	50		101	55		91	38	27

TABLE 1b - DESCRIPTION OF MANN ACT VIOLATORS BY *PERCENT* AND GROUP FOR YEARS 1927-1937

Group	Marital Status[1]				Age				Race			Citizenship			Education			IQ[2]			Children[3]			Prior[4] Convictions			Sentence (Yrs)			Region Where[5] Prosecuted		
	S	M	Dv		16-19	20-29	30+		W	Blk		USA	Other		None	8th	9th+		50-75	76+		0	1-2	3+		None	1+		1-19	2-5		South	Midwest	Other
1(N=36)	31	25	44		42	39	19		97	3		100	—		89	11		69	31		61	22	17		92	8		78	22		75	19	6
2(N=25)	28	24	48		20	72	8		100	—		96	4		60	40		52	48		68	28	4		76	24		80	20		76	24	0
3(N=23)	30	30	40		9	82	9		96	4		100	—		70	30		74	26		96	4	0		70	30		78	22		74	13	13
4(N=72)	18	38	44		3	39	58		94	6		93	7		82	18		65	35		58	36	6		53	47		49	51		38	31	31
Total (N=156)	24	31	45		15	51	34		96	4		96	4		79	21		65	35		66	27	7		68	32		65	35		58	24	17

1. Women separated and widowed were counted in divorced category.
2. Women whose IQ was too low to test were counted in 50-75 category.
3. Children were often not dependent on their mother at time of her arrest, i.e., grown-up, living with father, living with other relatives. The number of women with any dependent children included: Group 1-12, Group 2-6, Group 3-1, and Group 4-19.
4. Prior convictions were usually for such related offenses as prostitution, running a house of prostitution, liquor law violations, and vagrancy.
5. States counted in southern region: Alabama, Arkansas, Florida, Georgia, Louisiana, Mississippi, North Carolina, South Carolina, Tennessee, Texas, Virginia, and West Virginia. Midwestern states included: Illinois, Indiana, Iowa, Michigan, Minnesota, Missouri, Ohio, and Wisconsin.

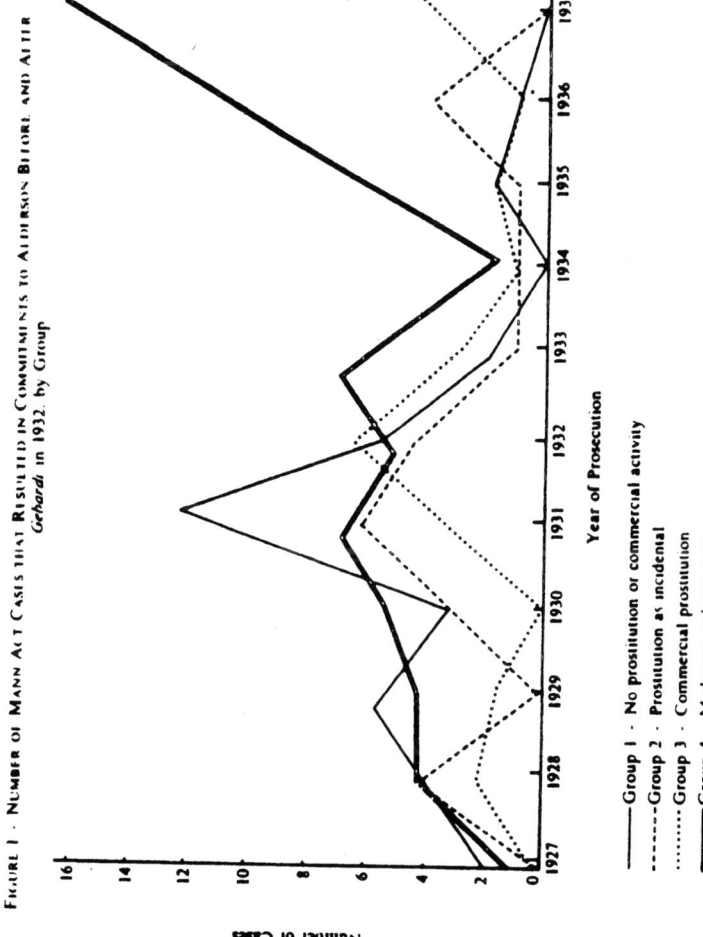

FIGURE 1. Number of Mann Act Cases that Resulted in Commitments to Alderson Before and After *Gebhard* in 1932, by Group

children. Of the total 156 women, only 38 had dependent children at the time of their arrest; aside from 9 with 3 or more dependents, 8 had 2 dependent children, and the remaining 21 had 1 dependent child. Almost all these women received low scores on the Binet Simon IQ test routinely administered by prison officials with 102 (65%) scoring below 76. Thirty-four (21%) went beyond the eighth grade in school.[29]

In contrast to the disproportionately black prison population in this country today, 150 (96%) of the women in the sample are white. Of the six black women, one became infatuated with a white fireman who took her from Montgomery, Alabama, to Columbus, Ohio, where they lived as man and wife until they were arrested. The second was the illegitimate daughter of a white prostitute mother and black father; she too became a prostitute to support her lover. The remaining four black women were madames—one was 63 years old.[30]

Despite the anxiety over "widespread prostitution by alien women," only six women were not U.S. citizens and of those, five were procurers. The sixth was a Mexican woman who most closely resembles the lawmakers stereotype of a "victim." The woman did not speak a word of English and was forced to commit acts of prostitution by her boyfriend, who held her captive by pocketing the money she earned and in return gave her gifts of inexpensive jewelry. Not only did this woman receive a prison sentence, she was also deported.[31]

Overall, the family histories of these women reveal deprived life experiences. Typically, the woman left home at an early age (i.e., 13 or 14) to enter a bad marriage or take on a menial job in the city. She sought to escape abusive parents who had forced her to quit school, or desolate rural surroundings. In many cases, her father or mother died when she was very young, and she had to take care of the surviving parent and a large number of even younger siblings. Most of these women were unskilled and had little education. They were, for the most part, law-abiding individuals. Only 16 women of a total of 84 in the first 3 groups had any prior convictions.[32] The following three case histories exemplify this pattern:

> When Leota's father became deputy sheriff in 1926, he began to drink liquor, deserted his family several times and repeatedly beat his wife and children. Leota's mother did washing, ironing and sewing in order to support herself and

the children. Leota made good grades and wanted to complete high school, but her father would not allow her to continue school after she was fourteen. Leota did the housework and took care of her younger brother and sister while her mother worked. Several times her father left the family without food and money and would be gone for weeks at a time. In 1928 he lost his position and took work now and then on the highway. He would come home at all hours and if supper was not ready, he would threaten to kill his wife. One night Leota heard her father threaten to kill her mother if she didn't get the salt shaker for him. After her mother got it, he threw his plate full of hot food at her. Leota ran to a neighbor's house and called the police who came and put her father in jail. When he was released on bond, he beat Leota and the other children everytime he came home from work. When Leota's sweetheart came and found her in tears, he begged her to marry him. She consented and left for Louisiana to get married since it took several days to get a license in Texas. Leota admits having immoral relations on the road. As soon as Leota's father learned that she was going to get married, he notified the police. She was arrested two weeks later.

Betty is the 7th of 15 children. Her childhood was very unhappy due to the family's poverty and her father's drinking liquor. Three siblings starved to death when they were infants. The father was never very ambitious and never provided a good home. Her parents and their five small children live in a one room shack and are considered "white trash." Betty finished the 5th grade and then ran away from home because her father was drunk and beat her often. She went to a tourist camp and worked for $10.00/week making beds and running errands. She sent this money to her mother and prostituted for her spending money. Betty has prostituted since she was 12 years of age. She was only 16 years old at the time of this arrest.

Ruby's mother died in childbirth when Ruby's father refused to call a doctor. He seemed repentant for a short while, then deserted the children. Ruby and her two young brothers shifted for themselves. Ruby had been going with a man by the name of Elmer. He was married, but separated from his wife and was expecting to divorce. After Ruby's father deserted the children, Ruby completed the 8th grade by living with Elmer's mother and working for her room and board. Elmer asked her to take a trip with him to Stubenville, Ohio promising that they would be gone only a few days. His mother thought it was okay for Ruby to go. Ruby had immoral relations with Elmer and lived with him for several days. When Elmer's wife learned that Elmer had taken Ruby across the state line, she reported it to the F.B.I. and they were both arrested for Mann Act violations.

In sum, the evidence shows that the women committed to Alderson for Mann Act violations were neither the helpless, naive, exploited "white slaves" of the Progressive Era imagination nor the independent, economically sophisticated, self-determining women the *Holte* Court believed them to be. The truth is somewhere in between. In reality, the female "violators" of the Mann Act were "victims" of their own hard lives and the morals of the time.

THE PRESENT STATUS OF THE MANN ACT

Law enforcement authorities have become less enthusiastic about enforcing a law which has grown increasingly unpopular with changes in sexual mores over the years. The U.S. National Archives and Records Service has prepared a historical narrative of the White Slave Traffic Act, based on extensive review of F.B.I. headquarters records. The narrative reports that:

> In 1962 the Department of Justice prohibited U.S. Attorneys from prosecuting noncommercial cases without express approval of the Criminal Division. The F.B.I. followed suit relying on local authorities to handle routine cases and concentrating on "organized commercialized prostitution." It is currently a low priority in F.B.I. field offices.[33]

Nonetheless, men and women are still being sent to prison for Mann Act violations. According to federal prison system records, 439 defendants were committed to federal prisons between 1970 and 1982 for violations of the act, 35 of whom are women. Although a review of the records of all 35 women most recently convicted is beyond the scope of this paper, it is reasonable to assume from post-*Gebardi* trends that these women more closely resemble the violators whom Congress had in mind when the statute was enacted. While these women are more likely to be madames or procurers of other women for prostition, they are not any more likely than their predecessors to be part of an organized white slave ring. Moreover, even though the Mann Act has decreased in use as a penal law, Congress has breathed new life into it. In 1978 the act was amended to make the interstate transportation of minor boys for sexual purposes a crime.[34] Whether this recent expression of legislative intent to protect young males will result in the same kinds of distortions by courts and enforcement agencies remains to be seen.

REFERENCES

1. The White Slave Traffic Act, ch. 395, 36 Stat. 825 (1910) (codified as amended at 18 U.S.C. §§ 2421-2424 (1976 and Supp. V 1981), includes this provision: "That any person who shall knowingly transport or cause to be transported, or aid or assist in obtaining transportation for, or in transporting, in interstate or foreign commerce . . . any woman or girl for the purpose of prostitution or debauchery, or for any other immoral purpose, or with the intent and purpose to induce, entice, or compel such woman or girl to become a prostitute or to give herself up to debauchery, or to engage in any other immoral practice; . . . shall be deemed guilty of a felony, and upon conviction thereof shall be punished by a fine not exceeding five thousand dollars, or by imprisonment of not more than five years; or by both such fine and imprisonment, in the discretion of the court."

2. According to Vern and Bonnie Bullough, *Prostitution: An Illustrated Social History* (New York: Crown Publishers, Inc., 1978), p. 245, the term "White Slavery" is often attributed to Clifford G. Roe, an Assistant State's Attorney in Illinois and a leader in the fight against involuntary prostitution. Roe supposedly used the term at the beginning of the twentieth century when he became involved in a case in which a girl had thrown a note from a house of prostitution. She had written: "Help me—I am held captive as a white slave." The incident may have occurred, but the term predated Roe's use. The term also comes from the English translation of the French term, "Traite des Blanches," trade in whites, used in Paris in 1902 at a conference of 15 European nations to discuss the problem of international trade in women and children. At an earlier international conference on the Negro slave trade, the French had used the phrase "Traite des Noires," trade in blacks, and the reference to white trade was used to contrast the later conference with the earlier one. The British Government translated the French term as "White Slave Traffic or Trade," and in the United States, this translation was usually abbreviated to "White Slavery."

3. E. Feldman, "Prostitution, the Alien Woman and the Progressive Imagination," *American Quarterly* 19 Summer (1967) 2, part I: 200, reports that between 1890 and 1900 the *Reader's Guide to Periodical Literature* lists 36 entries under the separate subject of "Prostitution"; between the years 1910 and 1914 entries climbed sharply to 156 and then dropped to 41, 1915-1924.

4. Alan Block, "Aw! Your Mother's in the Mafia: Women Criminals in Progressive New York," in *The Criminology of Deviant Women*, ed. Freda Adler and Rita Simon (Boston: Houghton, Mifflin, 1979), p. 180.

5. On December 10, 1909, the immigration commissioner made a personal appearance before Congress to testify about the prosecutions initiated by immigration agents against pimps and procurers. In his introduction the Commissioner referred to the importing and harboring of alien women and girls for immoral purposes and the practice of prostitution or the

so-called "white slave traffic" as the most pitiful and revolting phase of the immigration problem. The commissioner painted a lurid picture of the capture of young girls who were subsequently forced into lives of squalor and prostitution.

Eleven days after the commissioner's testimony, Representative Mann reported from committee the bill that Congress subsequently enacted as the White Slave Traffic Act. The purpose of the bill as stated in the House report includes the following: "[The Act] does not attempt to regulate the practice of voluntary prostitution, but aims solely to prevent panders and procurers from compelling thousands of women and girls against their will and desire to enter and continue in a life of prostitution." Representative Mann defined the term "white slave" to include "only those women and girls who are literally slaves—those women who are owned and held as property and chattels. . . those women and girls who, if given a fair chance, would, in all human probability, have been good wives and mothers and useful citizens."

6. Representative Mann emphasized that the intent of Congress was "not to interfere with or usurp in any way the police powers of the states." He stated that "the punishment of the practice of prostitution or the keeping of houses of ill-fame, or other immoral places, in the several states, are matters wholly within the powers of the states. . . ." This distinction made by Representative Mann between the aims of the act and "ordinary prostitution" was an important one. Power to enact this legislation was derived from the commerce clause and extended only to interstate criminal activity. Mann and others justified this early interstate crime by analogizing the transportation of women (who, if the rhetoric is to be taken at face value, were viewed as passive, nonvolitional victims) to the interstate transportation of goods for commercial purposes.

7. 242 U.S. 470, 485 (1917). Factors unique to the circumstances of *Caminetti* may have led to the prosecution and conviction of the defendants. First, the interstate weekend was not a casual affair, but rather the culmination of the seduction of two young women, aged 19 and 20, by married men in a situation not entirely free from coercion. The men had apparently concealed their marital and parental status from the women. When the women discovered the truth, the men allegedly induced the women to take the trip to Reno by telling them that their wives would prosecute them in the juvenile court if they were found out. Second, the case had political overtones. Representative Mann and his Republican colleagues were eager to direct national attention to the fact that one of the seducers was Drew Caminetti, the son of the Democratic commissioner of immigration.

8. 329 U.S. 14 (1946).
9. *Athanasaw v. United States*, 227 U.S. 326 (1913).
10. *Carey v. United States*, 265 F. 515 (8th Cir. 1920).
11. *Jarabo v. United States*, 158 F.2d 509 (1st Cir. 1946).
12. *MacKreth v. United States*, 103 F.2d 495 (5th Cir. 1939).
13. *United States v. Holte*, 236 U.S. 140 (1915); *Diggs v. United States*, 220 F. 545 (1915).
14. *Holte* at 145 (emphasis added).
15. 287 U.S. 112 (1932). The *Gebardi* Court left open the question of just how much activity over and above mere acquiescence would bring the woman's conduct within the ban of the statute.
16. William Seagle, "The Twilight of the Mann Act," 55 *American Bar Association Journal* 643 (1969).
17. U.S., Department of Justice Circular No. 647, issued January 26, 1917. From the beginning, the department has advised district attorneys: "As to specific cases, the Department must rely upon the discretion of the District Attorneys who have firsthand knowledge of the facts, and opportunity for personal interviews with the witnesses, and who will thus be able to ascertain what circumstances of aggravation, if any, attend the offense, the age and relative interest of the parties, the motives of those urging prosecution, and what reasons, if any, exist for thinking the ends of justice will be better served by a prosecution under Federal law than under the laws of the State having jurisdiction."
18. 1939 and 1940 are the only years for which conviction statistics contain a breakdown

of defendants and victims by both age and sex and whether commercial activity was involved. Fiscal year 1939 data show that out of a total of 425 cases, 88 did not involve commercial interstate activity. In 1940, the total cases numbered 415, of which 106 were not commercial interstate situations.

19. U.S., Department of Justice Circular No. 647, issued January 26, 1917.

20. For example, U.S., Department of Justice Circular No. 986, issued August 5, 1919; U.S., Department of Justice Circular No. 2027, issued April 19, 1929.

21. F.B.I. Policy Memorandum No. 66-6200-31 issued September 15, 1949, and titled "Policy and Procedure: White Slave Traffic Act," p. 10.

22. *Ibid.* at 41.

23. U.S., Department of Justice Circular No. 2347, issued December 14, 1932.

24. With regard to convictions of women F.B.I. data show that in fiscal year 1939 of a total of 429 defendants *committed* for commercial trafficking, 93 were female; out of 88 defendants *committed* where there was no evidence of commercialism, 6 were women. In 1949, of the 357 defendants *committed* for commercial trafficking, 49 were female, and out of 106 defendants committed where there was no commercialism, none were female. No sex comparison data is available for the years prior to the *Gebardi* decision.

25. This particular 10-year span was selected because of the special interest in noting the after-effects of the 1932 *Gebardi* case on subsequent convictions of women. There were a total of 179 Mann Act commitments to Alderson during this period. Twenty-three records were unavailable (i.e., missing or incomplete); therefore the study deals with the 156 cases for which information is available.

26. Although this information is self-reported, there are two checks on accuracy. First, the inmate had already been sentenced and was incarcerated and therefore had little to gain by being untruthful to institutional social workers. Second, the information reported was corroborated by a description of the circumstances of the offense completed by the prosecuting official and included in the inmate's file for later determination of parole eligibility.

27. U.S., National Archives, Department of Justice, Bureau of Prisons, Record Group Number 129, Alderson Inmate Case Files, 1927-1940.

28. *Ibid.*

29. *Ibid.*

30. *Ibid.*

31. *Ibid.*

32. *Ibid.*

33. Brief for Plaintiff at Appendix X, Vol. II, Category 31, n.p., *American Friends Service* v. *Webster*, No. 79-1655 (D.D.C., Appendix filed Jan. 8, 1982). This appendix is an appraisal of the records of the F.B.I. submitted to the court by the National Archives and Records Service.

34. Pub. L. No. 95-225, § 3, 92 Stat. 7, 8-9 (1978) (codified at 18 U.S.C. § 2423 (1982)).

New York State's Prostitution Statute: Case Study of the Discriminatory Application of a Gender Neutral Law

Frances P. Bernat

ABSTRACT. In 1978, New York State upgraded its "patronizing a prostitute" statute from a violation to a misdemeanor offense. It was expected that upgrading the law would accomplish essentially two goals: deter prostitution by giving the police incentive to arrest patrons, and end the disparity that existed between the prostitution and patronizing statutes, as prostitution had been a misdemeanor offense since 1969. These goals were not accomplished. An analysis of prostitution arrest information from Buffalo, New York, for the years 1977 through 1980, shows that the Buffalo city police arrest practices did not change despite the 1978 reform of the prostitution statute. In particular, women continued to be singled out for prostitution arrests more often than men. In addition, despite constitutional prohibition of gender based discrimination, New York State courts have not been persuaded to find unconstitutional the differential enforcement practices of the prostitution statute. One Buffalo criminal court, for example, approved gender based discrimination on the basis of insufficient police staffing. The end result was that while the new statute was to be gender neutral, the application of the law was not; police nonenforcement of patron activity perpetuated discrimination against women.

PART I: INTRODUCTION

Prostitution is a crime in almost every area of the United States,[1] and will most likely continue to be criminalized. In New York State, prostitution constitutes an offense when a "person engages or agrees or offers to engage in sexual conduct with another person in

---

Frances P. Bernat, J.D., is Assistant Professor of Political Science, Criminal Justice Program, Washington, State University at Pullman, 99164-4880. Special thanks are extended to Ms. Lee Gagnon, Director of the Buffalo City Court Records Room, who provided me with access to the records utilized in this study.

return for a fee."[2] Both women and men can be, and have been, arrested for prostitution. In addition to proscribing prostitution, New York State also prohibits patronizing a prostitute;[3] patronizing constitutes an offense when a person engages or agrees or offers to engage in sexual conduct with another person, or a third party, in return for paying a fee.[4]

Reform of the prostitution statute occurred in 1967, 1969 and 1978. The reforms were designed to penalize prostitution and patronizing in order to deter prostitution.

Prior to September 1, 1967, prostitution and patronizing a prostitute were incorporated into the vagrancy statute as violations, or noncriminal offenses. At that time, vagrancy was punishable by a sentence of up to six months of imprisonment.[5] Subsequently, following a penal law revision in 1967, both prostitution and patronizing were separately classified as violations, punishable by a maximum of 15 days imprisonment.[6]

For the next one and one/half years, law enforcement officials and prosecutors intensively lobbied the state legislature to reform the prostitution law.[7] The lobbying efforts focused on increasing penalties for prostitution, not patronizing. Lobbyists argued that if prostitution was not criminalized as a class A misdemeanor, the most serious misdemeanor offense, prostitution would run rampant in the large cities within the state and that the statute would have little deterrent effect.[8] However, the penal law review committee, the New York State's Senate Committee on Codes, decided otherwise. In 1969, the legislature made prostitution a class B misdemeanor for three reasons:

> First, the Committee believed that the Penal Law Commission's decision to make prostitution a violation had been well-considered and that the Law had been in effect too short a time for any group to be able to evaluate its effectiveness. Second, the Committee feared that giving prostitutes one year sentences would overcrowd the jails. Third, the senators on the Committee did not believe that the act of prostitution warranted a one year jail sentence.[9]

With respect to patronizing, lobbyists did not argue against proscribing patronizing as a violation.[10] On September 1, 1969, prostitution was made a class B misdemeanor,[11] while patronizing a prostitute remained as a violation.[12] As a result, prostitutes faced a maximum of three months imprisonment[13] while patrons faced a maximum of 15 days imprisonment.[14] Prostitutes were imprisoned for a longer period of time than patrons for essentially the same conduct.

During the years after the 1969 penal law reform, great pressure was brought on the New York State legislature by women's groups seeking to end the disparity in penalties between the prostitute and patron. It was asserted that the disparity existed between females and males because mostly females were arrested and, therefore, subjected to the harsher penalties of the prostitution statute. Almost a decade later, the legislature, responding to the pressure, reformed the law proscribing patron activity. On September 1, 1978, patronizing was upgraded from a violation to a class B misdemeanor.[15] In addition, the legislature enacted several other penal code sections which were designed to progressively increase the severity of the patron offense when young prostitutes were patronized.[16] In general, however, the statutory reform was designed to provide the same penalties for prostitution and for patronizing.

Since patronizing a prostitute is a crime, the 1978 reform of the patronizing law might have given law enforcement officials the incentive to arrest patrons as well as prostitutes to curb prostitution. This paper focuses on the 1978 criminal law revision of the prostitution statute to ascertain whether the objectives of the reform reflected the actual results of the reform. Specifically, this paper will analyze the legal parameters of prostitution and patronizing activity, and the distinctions made between conduct committed by females and that committed by males. It is expected that despite the statutory change in 1978, law enforcement officers did not alter their arrest practices and continued to arrest female prostitutes more often than male patrons. I argue that such an enforcement practice is unconstitutional. This study addresses law enforcement of the prostitution statute in Buffalo, New York, for the years 1977, 1978, 1979 and 1980.[17] Buffalo was selected as the location of the study for three reasons. First, it is the second largest urban area in New York State. Second, arrest records were available. Finally, there were court challenges to the constitutionality of the prostitution statute and its enforcement. Besides the data collected, court decisions which focused on the issue of selective enforcement of the prostitution statute will be analyzed.

PART II: BUFFALO LAW ENFORCEMENT OF THE NEW YORK STATE PROSTITUTION STATUTE

Over the past few years, the judicial system in New York State has been asked to determine the constitutionality of the state's enforcement practice of its prostitution laws. A state's enforcement practice is unconstitutional if it violates equal protection principles.[18] To show an unconstitutional enforcement practice, such as selective enforcement of a law, a criminal defendant must prove that: 1) the statute was not applied to others who were similarly situated with the defendant; and 2) the enforcement practice was based on impermissable criteria.[19] When alleging selective enforcement, part of the defendant's burden of proof within the first criteria of such an allegation is to prove that "conscious, intentional discrimination" exists.[20] Intentional discrimination against a particular group may be shown by statistical evidence "of a grossly disproportionate incidence of nonenforcement against others similarly situated. . . ."[21] As indicated above, this paper focuses on the arrest practices in Buffalo, New York, after the 1978 reform equalized the penalties, to determine if the statute was selectively enforced against prostitutes as opposed to patrons. Two categories of persons arrested for prostitution activity will be discussed: female prostitute arrestees and male patron arrestees.

An analysis of whether the Buffalo police selectively enforced the prostitution statute must concentrate on the differences, if any, between females arrested for prostitution and males arrested for patronizing, rather than between females and males arrested for prostitution. This is because a very small number of male prostitutes "work the streets," while there are larger numbers of female prostitutes and male patrons.[22] A conservative estimate of the number of prostitute to patron arrestees should be one to three, because it is estimated that prostitutes could generally service three customers each night. This estimate was obtained by looking at the number of arrests of males for patronizing made by Buffalo's vice squad on nights when the squad performed "Operation Johnny." "Operation Johnny" was a police undercover operation. A female police officer posed as a prostitute to effectuate the arrest of potential patrons of prostitutes. From 1977 through 1980, two or three female decoy officers were staked out for two or three hours a night about once a month. Despite the limited amount of time put into "Operation Johnny" by the Buffalo vice squad, the female officers were each able to arrest about three customers each night. In fact, almost all the arrests of patrons in Buffalo, from 1977 through 1980, occurred during the vice squad's "Operation Johnny."

When the nature of prostitution is considered, we should expect to find more patrons than prostitutes. Prostitutes service areas where the greatest number of patrons are likely to be located. Their objective is to service a patron quickly, return to the street and quickly attract another customer. This objective is motivated by both the need to make money and the desire not to be arrested for loitering.

As Table 1 shows, between 1977 and 1980, the majority of those arrested under the prostitution statute were women. Women prostitutes comprised 72.08% of the arrests in 1977, 76.90% in 1978, 81.54% in 1979, and 75.62% in 1980.[23] Male patrons comprised 22.84% of the arrests in 1977, 12.87% in 1978, 7.71% in 1979, and 14.69% in 1980. Overall, from 1977 through 1980, female prostitute arrestees comprised 77.39% of the arrests for prostitution activity. Male patron arrestees comprised 13.13% of the arrests in Buffalo between 1977 and 1980. These figures show that the Buffalo police focused their enforcement of the sex neutral prostitution statute primarily against women.

Even these figures may be a faulty indicator of the actual arrest percentage difference between female prostitute arrestees and male

TABLE 1

NUMBER AND PERCENT OF ARRESTS FOR PROSTITUTION ACTIVITY IN BUFFALO, NEW YORK (BY SEX AND YEAR) *

Year	Female Prostitution (NYPL §230.00)		Male Prostitution (NYPL §230.00)		Male Patronising a Prostitute (NYPL §230.00)		Total
	N	%	N	%	N	%	N
1977	142	72.08	10	5.08	45	22.84	197
1978	263	76.90	35	10.23	44	12.87	342
1979	349	81.54	46	10.75	33	7.71	428
1980	242	75.26	31	9.69	47	14.69	320
Total	996	77.39	122	9.48	169	13.13	1287

Source: Buffalo Police Department Cell Block and City Court Record Sheets: 1977-1980.
*Female Patrons, 0 throughout.

patron arrestees because the police in Buffalo also arrested persons for "loitering for the purposes of prostitution."[24] A person may be arrested for "loitering for the purposes of prostitution" if that person "remains or wanders about in a public place and repeatedly beckons to, or repeatedly stops, or repeatedly attempts to stop motor vehicles, or repeatedly interferes with the free passage of other persons, for the purpose of prostitution, or of patronizing a prostitute. . ."[25] An analysis of persons arrested for prostitution offenses, together with persons arrested for the "loitering" offense would provide a better indication of the differences between the percentage of women as compared to men who were arrested for prostitution activity. The combination of arrest statistics would show whether women were singled out for prostitution arrests regardless of the form—prostitution or loitering—taken by the prostitution activity. (Table 2.)

TABLE 2

NUMBER AND PERCENT OF COMBINED ARRESTS FOR PROSTITUTION ACTIVITY AND LOITERING FOR THE PURPOSES OF PROSTITUTION IN BUFFALO, NEW YORK (BY SEX AND YEAR)

Year	Female Prostitution and Female Loitering for the Purposes of Prostitution (N.Y.P.L §§230.00, 240.37)		Male Patronizing a Prostitute and Male Loitering for the Purposes of Prostitution* (N.Y.P.L. §§230.03, 240.37)		Total
	N	%	N	%	N
1977	355	84.52	65	15.48	420
1978	626	86.58	97	13.42	723
1979	583	90.67	60	9.33	643
1980	357	84.20	67	15.80	424
Total	1921	86.92	289	13.08	2210

Source: Buffalo Police Department Cell Block and City Court Record Sheets: 1977-1980.

*The number of male patrons is overestimated because the loitering arrests (§240.37) listed on the Cell Block Sheets make no indication whether the male was engaging in patron or prostitution activity. Since females were not arrested for patron activity during the period studies, it is assumed that the loitering females were arrested for prostitution activity rather than patron activity.

Arrest figures show that women were arrested for the combined offenses of prostitution and loitering 84.52% of the time in 1977, 86.58% of the time in 1978, 90.67% of the time in 1979, and 84.20% of the time in 1980. In contrast, the arrest figures show that male patrons were arrested for combined activities of patronizing and loitering 15.48% of the time in 1977, 13.42% of the time in 1978, 9.33% of the time in 1979, and 15.80% of the time in 1980.[27] Overall, we can see that women comprised 86.92% of the combined offense arrests, while men comprised 13.08% of such arrests between 1977 and 1980. Once again, despite the fact there are believed to be greater numbers of patrons than prostitutes, prostitution laws were almost always enforced against women rather than men.

All the above findings are disturbing. They show a disproportionate percentage of women arrested for prostitution activity, and also that the new patron statute did not alter enforcement practices of the police. When police resources are scarce, as they were in Buffalo, concentration on criminal activity takes precedence over noncriminal activity. After the promulgation of the upgraded patron statute in 1978, one might have expected to find an increase in the proportion of men arrested for patronizing, because police would have had more incentive to arrest patrons for a crime than for a violation.[28] This expectation proved incorrect. Instead, the percentage of men arrested for patronizing in 1978 and 1979 decreased from 1977, while the percentage of women arrested for prostitution increased for the same period.

The increased arrests for patrons in 1980 is misleading for two reasons: 1) during the summer of 1980, when enforcement of the prostitution statute was constitutionally challenged in Buffalo City Court in *People v Burton*[29] pressure was placed on Buffalo police to enforce the patron law; and 2) during the end of 1980, the Buffalo police overall instituted a work slow-down which appears to have affected the number of arrests for female prostitution throughout the last months of the year.

In the *Burton* case, Burton, a criminal defendant, was arrested for "loitering for the purposes of prostitution." Her patron was not arrested. The court in *People v Burton*, 1980, was asked to determine whether the Buffalo police were selectively enforcing the prostitution statute against women, despite reform of the law proscribing patron activity. In June 1980, the court held a hearing on the selective enforcement issue. In addition to the factual circumstances surrounding her arrest, Burton presented statistical evidence of the disproportionate number and percentage of women arrested for prostitution and for "loitering for the purposes of prostitution" in Buffalo from 1977 through June 1980.[30] On September 12, 1980, the *Burton* court handed down its decision, holding the unequal enforcement of the statute to be constitutional.[31]

To determine if the hearing placed pressure on local enforcement of the prostitution statute, one must review the number of arrests for patronizing a prostitute. The patron arrest data reveals that of a total of 47 men arrested in the year 1980, 31 of these arrests (66%) occurred between June and September, the time period when the local criminal court in Buffalo was conducting its hearing and decided the selective enforcement issue. It is, therefore, conceivable that the court case placed immediate pressure on the police to maintain a high number of patronizing arrests.

Also, during the last few months of 1980, an internal dispute arose between police officers and the Buffalo Police Department and city. The police officers' contract with the city was under negotiation. Unhappy with the way labor negotiations were progressing, officers instituted a work slow-down. The slow-down resulted in fewer women arrested for prostitution during the last quarter, September through December, of 1980. If we compare the number of arrests of female prostitutes during September through December for each of the years discussed in this paper, 1977 - 1980, we find that significantly fewer women were arrested during the work slow-down time period in 1980. Specifically, in 1977, 68 women were arrested for prostitution in the September through December time period, 97 women in 1978, 91 women in 1979, and 47 women in 1980. Had the slow-down not occurred, one would have expected that the pattern of the previous three years would continue and more women, possibly twice as many, would have been arrested during the last quarter of 1980.

The slow-down did not effect the number of men arrested for patronizing during the last quarter of 1980. Specifically, in 1977, 45 men (all of the patron arrests for 1977) were arrested for patronizing in the September through December time period, 16 men in 1978, 10 men in 1979, and 12 men in 1980. With the exception of 1977, the number of arrests remained more or less constant. Arguably, the *Burton* case might have effected the number of patron arrests during the last quarter of 1980. As indicated above, the Buffalo police effectuated most of their arrests in 1980 during the June through

September time period. However, even if the number of arrests for patronizing during the last quarter of each year studied excluded the month of September, the police went about their business as usual. Specifically, in 1977, 17 men were arrested for patronizing in the October through December time period, 4 men in 1978, 1 man in 1979, and 1 man in 1980. Again, with the exception of 1977, the number of arrests for patronizing remained more or less constant.

In light of these two factors, the court case and the police work slow-down, the percentage of women as compared to men arrested under the prostitution statute in 1980 should be viewed as an anomaly, since both operated to inflate the percentage of males arrested for patronizing while deflating the percentage of females arrested for prostitution.

If the differences between the number and percentage of prostitution and patronizing arrests are to be compared by a court which has been asked to determine the constitutionality of the state's enforcement practice, the court must determine, or acknowledge, that prostitutes and patrons are similarly situated groups. If the groups are not similarly situated, then further constitutional review would be inappropriate, regardless of any statistical difference between the two groups' arrest rates. While the court in *People v Burton*, 1980, did not explicitly indicate that the two groups, prostitutes and patrons, were similarly situated, the court did allow a pre-trial hearing on the issue of selective enforcement of the prostitution statute against females and did compare the difference in arrest practices by the Buffalo police in regard to prostitutes and patrons. In addition, the court analyzed whether the state's reasons for the gross disparity between the percentage of prostitute and patron arrests were "good and sufficient."[32] Because such an analysis can occur only after the state has had an opportunity to rebut proof presented by a defendant in support of her/his claim, the court in *Burton* tacitly acknowledged that the categories are comparable.

Another criminal court in Syracuse, New York, explicitly held in 1980 in *People v Nelson*[33] that prostitutes and patrons are similarly situated groups. This holding, as to whether prostitutes can be compared with patrons by a court determining if there is unconstitutional enforcement of the prostitute statute, should have put to rest the issue of the statute's sections comparability; but, both the *Burton*, 1980, and *Nelson*, 1980, decisions can be contrasted with a New York appellate court decision, *In re Dora P.*,[34] 1979. In *In re Dora P.*, the court ruled that equal protection was not violated by the selective enforcement practices of the New York City police because the prostitution statute delineated the offense of prostitution and patronizing into two separate sections, N.Y.P.L. §230.00 and §230.03, respectively. The court, in *In re Dora P.*, held that two "separate crimes" could not be compared when an individual is alleging disparate treatment because the crimes require "separate acts... to affect their commission."[35] Local criminal courts in Buffalo are not required to follow the opinion in *In re Dora P.*, as it was not decided by the appellate division reviewing lower court decisions from Western New York. In 1981, however, a Buffalo criminal court adopted the analysis found in *In re Dora P.* and also held that prostitutes and patrons are not similarly situated persons.[36]

The court in *In re Dora P.* appears to argue that since two separate sections for prostitution and patronizing are provided by the prostitution law, they are not comparable. Yet, the "loitering for the purposes of prostitution" statute, defined above, does not separate the activity of patrons and prostitutes, as both acts are proscribed within a single statutory section. If the appellate court's concerns in *In re Dora P.* were appropriate or correct, then proscription of patronizing and prostitution could not be contained together within the single section of the loitering statute. Therefore, it is possible that the prostitution and patronizing sections of the prostitution statute could have been contained within a single statutory section, as the state legislature designed the loitering statute,[38] and may be comparable in a constitutional review.

To determine whether the two classes of people, prostitutes and patrons, are similarly situated, an understanding of the two sections of the prostitution statute is essential. Perhaps the only rational consideration for finding that the two sections are not comparable would be that the sections are dissimilar because they have different purposes and proscribe different acts. Historically, the New York legislature has repeatedly indicated that the purpose of proscribing prostitution and patronizing is to deter prostitution activity by reaching both the source, prostitutes, and the demand, patrons.

The issue as to whether the sections proscribe the same acts is much more difficult to answer. As argued above, the mere fact that the statute has separate sections does not necessarily mean that the sections are not comparable. Common sense indicates that while the prostitute and patron have different roles to be carried out when committing prostitution, the nature of the activity, commercial sex, is the same. The court in *People* v *Nelson*, 1980, specifically found that:

> The court in *Matter of Dora P.* also based its conclusion on its consideration of the "separate acts necessary to effect their commission," but did not mention what those separate acts were. If we compare §230.00 (prostitution) with §230.02 (patronizing a prostitute; definitions), we find that the only significant difference in the proscribed behavior is that the prostitute sells sex and the patron buys it. Neither gender nor solicitation is a differentiating factor.[37]

While a differentiation between the responsibilities and liabilities of sellers and buyers may occur when analyzing some crimes, the distinction is not easily made in regard to "sellers" and "buyers" of prostitution. For example, criminal liability usually falls heavier on sellers of narcotics than buyers because the seller is perceived to constitute a greater threat to the community. However, the New York legislature upgraded the patron law to acknowledge that patrons and prostitutes present similar, or the same, threats to the community. Prostitution activity by patrons and prostitutes may interfere with the free flow of traffic, or may involve the harassment of persons who are not prostitutes or their patrons. Because the activity of patrons and prostitutes might be described as a joint commercial venture with comparable or the same community consequences, such groups may be similarly situated.

By showing that the police in Buffalo were disproportionately arresting women for prostitution, and that prostitutes and patrons may be similarly situated groups, a case for gender based discrimination can be made. If the state cannot justify its enforcement practice, then such a practice is unconstitutional. In gender based discrimination situations, the state must prove that the enforcement practice bears a fair and *substantial relationship*, which is in the public interest, to an important state objective.[39] The heightened scrutiny test is the middle-tier of equal protection doctrine and makes it difficult for a state to justify semi-suspect classifications based on gender groups.

In *People* v *Burton*, 1980, the Buffalo court's findings of fact and law appear to be logical and just by balancing the defendant's allegation of discrimination with the state's reasons for its existence.

However, in constitutional analysis, the court did not utilize the substantial relationship test. Instead, the court considered whether the state had "good and sufficient reasons" for the unequal treatment of women.[41] In this regard, the *Burton* court specifically found:

> For one thing, the Buffalo Police Department is short of manpower in general, laboring under budgetary restrictions, which cannot be easily corrected, since they are due to a shrinking tax base and other problems common to older cities. For another, the police department is guilty of engaging in discriminatory hiring practices of women in the past, it has very few women on its force, and it is now under a federal court mandate to increase the number of women in the force. Therefore, when police decoys are needed (to arrest patrons of prostitutes), they must be obtained from other bureaus in the department outside the vice squad because they do not mesh with the other related duties of this squad, such as the prosecution of male prostitution, and of gambling and liquor law violations. Also, the use of police decoys requires additional manpower because the policewomen have to be guarded from prostitutes on the street where they are staked out and they must have additional back-up support to arrest sometimes panicky "Johns." For these reasons, police decoys are not as readily employed against male customers as male decoys or officers are against female prostitutes. For these reasons and others, it is more efficient to use police manpower to arrest female prostitutes than their male customers.[42]

The police enforcement practice of the state's prostitution statute was upheld in *Burton*, at least for the time being,[43] because of staffing problems. These practices were not found unconstitutional on the basis of gender discrimination.

A "good and sufficient reasons" test of constitutionality is a less strict standard of review than the substantial relationship test applied to cases of racial discrimination. A careful analysis of the *Burton* court's rationale for its decision would indicate that the court's reasons would not withstand the heightened scrutiny test.

The city's budgetary problems resulted in "manpower" shortages on the police force. In economically hard times, a police department has to effectively allocate its funds and resources so that the greater number of persons who commit crimes are apprehended. Which offenders the police should focus attention upon, prostitutes or patrons, is not easily answered. Prostitutes repeatedly return to the streets to service patrons, even after they are arrested and released on bail or bond. Because patrons do not return to the streets after they engaged the services of a prostitute, or are arrested, the choice might be to arrest the female. However, time and again, it has been found that police attempts to "sweep the streets" of prostitution by arresting prostitutes did not stop or deter prostitution.[44] Such police crackdowns only served to move prostitution to other locations in a city. The legislature, by enacting the patron law, has acknowledged that by attacking the demand, patronizing, cities might be better able to stop or deter prostitution. Simply stated, if there is no demand, there is no service. The patron law, as indicated above, is designed to give police incentive to arrest males in the battle against prostitution. If a male knows that police are arresting patrons, he might not want to risk the consequences stemming from an arrest. These consequences might be more than punishment for commission of a crime. In Buffalo during "Operation Johnny," for example, the names of patrons were published in local newspapers. Since males arrested for patron activity are usually white, middle class family men, it was hoped that men would not patronize prostitutes if they knew they, or their families, might be subject to public ridicule.[45]

The *Burton* court indicated that as a result of "manpower" shortages, difficulties arose in assigning female officers to the vice squad. These difficulties, according to the court, were due to employment discrimination in hiring practices, the inability of female officers to "mesh" with other vice squad duties, and the need for back-up support for female officers. These justifications stem from "archaic and overbroad" generalizations about the capabilities of women who perform police work. The equal protection clause is designed to curtail misconceptions "concerning females in the home rather than in the 'marketplace and world of ideas.'"[46]

Studies of the history of women in policing have shown that substantial discrimination did not end as more women were hired into the police ranks. For example, according to Clarice Feinman:

> In departments containing more than one precinct, women have to prove themselves over and over again in each precinct

to which they are assigned... Because there are so few women in each department, women tend to be transferred from one tour of duty or special assignment or precinct to another more frequently than men. Each time a woman is transferred she again has to go through the lonely process of proving her ability by working harder than men.[47]

Any temporary assignment of women for decoys to the vice squad, operated as a continual prohibitive factor to the acceptance of women on the squad. Women officers would be continually thought unable to fit into vice squad work, even if they were capable of performing these duties. Further, most male officers work with partners and, in Buffalo, vice squad officers working undercover as a "lone" patron in a car almost always have another officer waiting nearby to aid in the effectuation of the arrest. While some patrons do become "panicky," so, too, do some prostitutes. This back-up support for male decoy officers does not solve the problem of alleged "manpower" shortages. In addition, policewomen assigned to a decoy operation when one police department began a crackdown on prostitution in 1974 were physically able to defend themselves and effectuate arrests without any help.[48] Of more crucial importance, the *Burton* court's analysis appears to state that existing conditions, sexual discrimination against female police officers, justified the discrimination against another group of women, prostitutes.

As the court's scrutiny is intended to prevent the perpetuation of gender discrimination, courts should not allow a state's law enforcement practices to perpetuate it. A finding that "manpower" problems justified the disparity in arrests between women and men (prostitutes and patrons) should not be upheld.

PART III: CONCLUSION

In New York State, prostitution and patronizing a prostitute are crimes of equal severity, class B misdemeanors. Prior to September, 1978, patronizing was a non-criminal offense, a violation; prostitution has been a crime since 1969. In 1978, the state legislature upgraded the patron offense: Both prostitutes and patrons of prostitutes were to be treated alike by state enforcement officials in efforts to deter prostitution. This paper has analyzed whether enforcement of the New York State prostitution statute in one major city, Buffalo, was selective despite reform of the prostitution statute.

This inquiry consisted of analysis of two issues: whether the enforcement practice was selective, and whether the enforcement practice was based upon an impermissable criterion, gender. An enforcement practice may be constitutionally impermissible if it intentionally treats similar situated groups differently. It has been shown that a disproportionate percentage of women, as compared to men, were arrested for prostitution. If the party alleging selective enforcement does not prove intentional discrimination, then the state practice would presumably be found constitutional. Additionally, it was argued that prostitutes and patrons are similarly situated groups because the two sections of the prostitution statute have the same purpose and proscribe the same acts.

Gender is a classification that will receive heightened scrutiny if harmful gender based discrimination has been alleged. To date, no New York court has utilized the appropriate test when determining if the state's prostitution enforcement practice has been constitutional. A state practice based on gender must bear a fair and substantial relationship to a legitimate state interest, and must be in the public interest. Once intentional discrimination is proved, such a test can make it difficult for a state to defend selective enforcement practices. The state's argument that it has "manpower" problems hindering its enforcement in Buffalo of the prostitution statute seems unlikely to pass constitutional muster. The Buffalo police were basically operating as if the old patron law were in effect. Regardless of increased incentive to arrest persons committing a criminal offense, as opposed to those engaging in noncriminal behavior, the Buffalo police concentrated arrest efforts on females, the prostitutes. Because in *Burton* the Buffalo City Court did not hold unconstitutional the selective enforcement practice, gender based discrimination was perpetuated. Women were thereby placed in a double bind. Because there was discrimination in hiring women onto the police force and no women were assigned to the vice squad, the police were allowed to focus their arrests on female prostitution. Although there was a gender neutral prostitution statute in New York State, there was no gender neutral enforcement of the statute. Because selective enforcement of the prostitution statute kept women in a vulnerable position, a continued assessment of prostitution arrest practices by the police in Buffalo, or elsewhere, is essential. Although Buffalo is the only city in New York State where prostitution arrest data have been collected,[49] similar enforcement practices may exist in other cities. The objective of penal law reform may be to end past inequities, but deeply ingrained practices of gender based discrimination are difficult to curtail.

REFERENCES

1. The State of Nevada allows prostitution in unincorporated areas (less than 200,000 population). Nev. Rev. Stats. §269.175 (1979).
2. N.Y.P.L. §230.00 (McKinney 1980).
3. N.Y.P.L. §§230.03, 230.04, 230.05, 230.06 (McKinney 1980).
4. N.Y.P.L. §230.02 (McKinney 1980)
5. Former Code of Criminal Procedure §887(4) (McKinney Practice Commentary. N.Y.P.L. §230.00, 1980); People v Bailey, 432 N.Y.S. 2d 789 (N.Y. City Crim. Ct., 1980).
6. N.Y.P.L. §230.00 (McKinney Practice Commentary 1980).
7. Pamela Roby, "Politics and Criminal Law: Revision of the New York State Penal Law and Prostitution," Social Problems 17 (Summer 1969): 102-03.
8. N.Y.P.L. §230.00 (McKinney Practice Commentary 1980).
9. Roby, "Politics and the Criminal Law," p. 103.
10. Ibid., p. 101.
11. N.Y.P.L. §230.00 (McKinney 1980).
12. N.Y.P.L. §230.03 (McKinney 1980).
13. N.Y.P.L. §70.15 (2) (McKinney 1980).
14. N.Y.P.L. §70.15 (4) (McKinney 1980).
15. N.Y.P.L. §230.03 (McKinney 1980).
16. N.Y.P.L. §230.04 (McKinney 1980) is a class A misdemeanor; N.Y.P.L. §230.05 (McKinney 1980) is a class E felony; N.Y.P.L. §230.06 (McKinney 1980) is a class D felony. In Buffalo, where this study was carried out, there were no arrests of patrons of minor prostitutes for the time period studied. Additionally, a defense to such a charge is that the patron did not know the age of the minor prostitute, N.Y.P.L. §230.07 (McKinney 1980). Therefore, it seems doubtful that these patron sections will effectively deter patrons from seeking young women for hire.
17. Data found earlier than 1977 were not retrieved by this researcher because they were not stored in an accessible manner. The data that were collected include one and one/half years of pre-patron statutory reform and one and one/half years of post-patron statutory reform.
18. In New York State, equal protection of the laws is guaranteed by the Fourteenth Amendment to the U.S. Constitution and by Article 1, §11 of the state constitution.
19. People v Goodman, 338 N.Y.S. 2d 97 (1972).
20. People v Nelson, 427 N.Y.S. 2d 194 (1980).
21. 427 N.Y.S. 2d 194, 198.
22. This author reviewed the arrest sheets on everyone arrested in the city of Buffalo from 1977 through 1980. Persons arrested for a prostitution related offense were identified by McKinney's N.Y.P.L. section numbers; i.e., an arrested person was spotted by a §230.00 penal code designation. Date of arrest, sex and charge were recorded.
Although it is difficult to give an exact number of the male and female prostitutes working in Buffalo from 1977 through 1980, an overall total of 996 arrests of women (89.09%), as opposed to a total of 122 arrests of men (10.91%), for prostitution occurred during that period. That fewer men than women were arrested for prostitution may be attributed to the fact there are not as many male as female prostitutes in the Buffalo area [People v Burton, 432 N.Y.S. 2d 312, 314 (1980)]. Therefore, male prostitution arrestees did not make up a large percentage of arrests overall. By year, in 1977, male arrestees comprised 5.08% of the

arrests, in 1978, 10.23%; in 1979, 10.75%; and, in 1980, 9.69% of the arrests. These male prostitute arrests were effected by undercover male police officers.

The male prostitution arrestee percentages roughly reflect the same increase/decrease trends indicated for female prostitution arrests. That is, between 1977 and 1979, prostitution arrests increased; but in 1980, prostitution arrests decreased.

23. There were no arrests for females patronizing a prostitute. This fact might be due to the scarcity of women patronizing prostitutes in the Buffalo, New York, area, or it might be due to the police's failure to focus on such activity.

24. N.Y.P.L. §240.37 (McKinney 1980).

25. N.Y.P.L. §240.37 (McKinney 1980); cited in *People* v *Smith*, 407 N.Y.S. 2d 462, 464-5 (1978).

26. Arrest data for males and females who were charged with "loitering for the purposes of prostitution" were collected in the same fashion as data collected on prostitution arrests: See footnote 22.

27. The combined male patron arrest figures may be inflated because arrest records utilized for the "loitering for the purpose of prostitution" offense made no distinction between male prostitution and male patron offenses. Thus, the combined male patron figures in Table 2 probably include male prostitution arrests.

28. Interview, Chief of Operations Robert Ford of the Erie County Sheriff's Department, Summer 1979.

29. 432 N.Y.S. 2d 312.

30. The statistical evidence presented a comparison of the number and percentage of males and females arrested for prostitution and loitering for the purposes of prostitution from 1977 to June 1980; basically, my data are presented in Tables 1 and 2.

31. Because of the complex legal issues involved, the decision will be analyzed in detail later in the text. In general, however, the court found that "although the circumstances of the defendant's arrest and the fact that almost all of the people arrested in Buffalo for prostitution-related offenses are women would seem to suggest that the defendant and other women are victims of bias, a comprehensive view satisfies this court that there are good and sufficient reasons . . . to justify . . ." the enforcement practice, 432 N.Y.S. 2d 312, 315.

32. 432 N.Y.S. 2d 312, 315 (1980).

33. 427 N.Y.S. 2d 194.

34. *In re Dora P.*, 418 N.Y.S. 2d 597 (1979).

35. 418 N.Y.S. 2d 597, 604.

36. *People* v *Simms*, No. 2C-50775, Buffalo City Court, Filed April 1, 1981.

37. 427 N.Y.S. 2d 194, 197.

38. Some states do proscribe patronizing and prostitution within the same statute: Fla. Stats. Ann. §796.07 a, b, e (1978 and 1982 Supp.); Iowa §725.1 (1979); Minn. Stats. Ann. §609.324 (1982 Supp.); N.J. Stats Ann. §26:34-1 a, e (West 1982); Ore. Rev. Stats. §167.007 (1981); Penn. Stats Ann. §18-5902 a, e (Purdon 1973).

39. *Craig* v *Boren*, 97 S. Ct. 451, 458 (1976); *California* v *Goldfarb*, 97 S. Ct. 1021 (1977); *Orr* v *Orr*, 99 S. Ct. 1102 (1979); *Mississippi University for Women* v *Hogan*, 102 S. Ct. 1422 (1982).

40. 432 N.Y.S. 2d 312, 314-315.

41. 432 N.Y.S. 2d 312, 315.

42. 432 N.Y.S. 2d 312, 315.

43. 432 N.Y.S. 2d 312. The *Burton* court did warn that "what may be good and sufficient reasons today will not suffice tomorrow when there are many more women available in the police ranks," at 315.

44. Jacqueline Boles and Charlotte Sadro, "Legal and Extra-Legal Methods of Controlling Female Prostitution: Cross-Cultural Comparison," *International Journal of Comparative and Applied Criminal Justice* 2 (Spring 1978) pp. 78-80; Holcome B. Noble, "A Return to the Old Morality Puts New Pressure on City Police," *Police Magazine* 2 (March 1979) pp. 55-56.

45. Frances P. Bernat, "Gender Disparity in the Setting of Bail: Prostitution Offenses in Buffalo, N.Y.: 1977-1979," *Journal of Offender Counseling, Services and Rehabilitation* 9 (forthcoming 1984).

46. *Craig v Boren*, 97 S. Ct. 451, 457-458 (1976). Also, *Califano v Goldfarb*, 97 S. Ct. 1021, 1029 (1977).

47. Clarice Feinman, *Women in the Criminal Justice System* (New York: Praeger, 1980), p. 79.

48. Susan Martin, *Breaking and Entering: Policewomen on Patrol* (Berkeley: University of California Press, 1980).

49. In *People v Nelson*, 427 N.Y.S. 2d 194, (1980), the court refused to allow the defendant access to the city's arrest records, thereby making it impossible for the defendant to prove selective enforcement of the prostitution statute in Syracuse, New York.

PART IV: CONTRIBUTOR'S CHOICES— ANNOTATED BIBLIOGRAPHY

Contributors were asked to recommend the resources they considered most helpful and critical to their areas. The annotated list below represents their choices.

Subject Area:
Domestic Violence—Battered Women

Recommendations of Janice Grau,
Jeffrey Fagan, and Sandra Wexler

Berk, R. A., and L. Sherman. *Final Report: The Specific Deterrent Effect of Arrest for Spouse Assault.* Washington, D.C.: The Police Foundation, 1983.

> The results of a three-year field experiment show that arrest is the most effective disposition in preventing subsequent abuse for police intervention in spouse assault cases. Arrest was superior to both informal adjustment or no action.

Field, M. H., and H. F. Field, "Marital Violence and the Criminal Process: Neither Justice nor Peace." *Social Service Review* 47, 1973: 221-240.

Grau, J. A. "Restraining Order Lesiglation for Battered Women: A Reassessment." *University of San Francisco Law Review* (1982), p. 16.

Lerman, L. G., and F. Livingston. "State Legislation on Domestic Violence," *Response* 6, September 1983: 1-28.

> This volume contains a comprehensive state-by-state listing of legislation pertaining to domestic violence, including the legal remedies for persons abused by family or household members

and the powers and duties of the police or courts which handle family violence cases.

Lerman, L. G. "Criminal Prosecution of Wife Beaters." *Response* 4, January 1981: 1-9.

> This article examines the practical problems involved in criminal prosecution of domestic violence cases. It reviews the historical objections to prosecution in light of empirical evidence on the characteristics of abusers and the efficacy of prosecution in stopping subsequent abuse.

Loving, N. *Responding to Spouse Abuse and Wife Beating: A Guide for Police.* Washington, D.C.: Police Executive Research Forum, 1980.

Parnas, R. "Prosecutorial and Judicial Handling of Family Violence." *Criminal Law Bulletin* 9, 1973.

Schecter, S. *Women and Male Violence: The Vision and Struggle of the Battered Women's Movement.* Boston: South End Press, 1982.

> The history of the battered women's movement is documented in this book. The emergence of wife abuse as a social problem and the organization of the battered women's social movement are traced. The book documents the accomplishments of the movement in providing shelter to its victims and altering the institutional responses of the social and legal agencies which serve battered women. The problems facing the movement are analyzed, including: financial constraints, a political backlash against feminism, and the need to develop professional but autonomous services. An agenda for ending wife abuse is proposed.

Straus, M. A., R. J. Gelles, and S. K. Steinmetz. *Behind Closed Doors: Violence in the American Family.* Garden City, N.Y.: Anchor, 1980.

> Based on interviews with 2,143 families, estimates of the incidence, prevalence, and severity of violence in families are developed. Predictors of child abuse and spousal violence are examined.

U. S. Commission on Civil Rights. *Under the Rule of Thumb: Battered Women and the Administration of Justice.* Washington, D.C.: U.S. Commission on Civil Rights, 1981.

Walker, L. E. *The Battered Woman.* New York: Harper, Row, 1979.

> This study of battered women includes an examination of the contributions of weak or inconsistent judicial responses to the development of violence between intimates and to "learned helplessness," a fundamental part of the "battered women syndrome."

Recommendations by Daisy Quarm and Martin D. Schwartz

Over the past decade, there has been a veritable explosion of both scholarly and popular literature on the subject of domestic violence and its several subtopics. Because of space limitations we have included only books and articles published since 1980 and two comprehensive bibliographies that review the literature appearing in 1980 or earlier.

Breines, Wini, and Linda Gordon. "The New Scholarship on Family Violence." *Signs* 8, 1983: 490-531.

> A review essay critically examining recent work in the areas of child abuse, battering, and incest from a socialist feminist perspective.

EMERGE. *EMERGE: A Men's Counseling Service on Domestic Violence.* Boston: EMERGE, 1981.

> Describes a counseling program for men who batter developed by an all-male collective that provides counseling for batterers. Their program is based on an analysis of battering which explicitly includes political, social, and economic factors which influence battering. Group counseling for batterers and community education designed to change social norms are both integral parts of the EMERGE program. Workshops for persons interested in starting programs for men who batter as well as written information is available from EMERGE (25 Huntington Avenue, Room 324, Boston, MA 02116; 617-267-7690).

Ganley, Anne L. *Court-Mandated Counseling for Men Who Batter: A Three-Day Workshop for Mental Health Professionals.* Washington, D.C.: Center for Women Policy Studies, 1981.

> Describes a counseling program for men who batter based on social learning theory. It avoids victim-blaming, but focuses

solely on helping individual batterers change their behavior and offers no strategies for attempting to change the societal factors which are the structural bases of battering.

Gelles, Richard. "Domestic criminal violence," in *Criminal Violence*, ed. Marvin E. Wolfgang and Neil A. Weiner. Beverly Hills, California: Sage, 1982, pp. 201-35.

An overview of both the latest empirical findings and theories in the literature, and also a guide to the specific academic journal articles dealing with various subtopics and issues.

Johnson, Carolyn, John Ferry, and Majorie Kravitz (Comps.). *Spouse Abuse: A Selected Bibliography*. Rockville, Maryland: National Criminal Justice Service, 1978.

A well-annotated bibliography of 55 items on the nature of the problem and 35 items on intervention, including conference papers, books, articles, and government reports, all from the mid-1970s. Included is information on how to obtain all items on microfiche or loan from the National Criminal Justice Reference Service.

Lerman, Lisa. *Prosecution of Spouse Abuse: Innovations in Criminal Justice Response*. Washington, D.C.: Center for Women Policy Studies, 1981.

A comprehensive review of attempts in various parts of the U.S. to improve the prosecution of spouse abuse cases. Includes data on the outcome of these innovations to the extent it is available.

Loving, Nancy. *Responding to Spouse Abuse and Wife Beating: A Guide for Police*. Washington, D.C.: Police Executive Forum, 1980.

Produced by an organization of large-city police chiefs, this book covers the nature of wife-beating and the problems of police response from a position sensitive to the problems and fears of the police.

Loving, Nancy. *Spouse Abuse: A Curriculum Guide for Police Trainers*. Washington, D.C.: Police Executive Forum, 1981.

This second book produced by the Police Executive Research Forum is designed for police agency trainers, and includes a complete 20-hour training course emphasizing not only police tactics, but also officer self-awareness of their own beliefs, and material placing policing in the large community context. It includes a good variety of resource materials designed explicitly for reproduction and distribution, and a course evaluation form.

Response.

This monthly newsletter published by the Center for Women Policy Studies (2000 P Street, N.W., Suite 508, Washington, D.C. 20036) is useful in keeping abreast of current literature on family violence. For example, the January/February 1982 issue reviews the recent literature concerning sheltering, counseling, social service advocacy, legal advocacy, medical advocacy, community education, volunteer training, rural programs, military programs, children's programs, programs for men who batter, and criminal justice programs.

Schechter, Susan. *Women and Male Violence: The Visions and Struggle of the Battered Women's Movement.* Boston: South End Press, 1982.

An examination of battering and the social movement against it, written from a socialist feminist perspective which views male dominance in the family and society as the fundamental cause of violence against women. The author bases her conclusions on case histories, historical documentation, and over 75 interviews with people from all parts of the country and from a wide range of organizations, as well as her own experience as an activist in both the anti-rape and battered women's movements in Chicago and on the East coast. Part I, which examines the history of the battered women's movement and records the contributions, cooperation, and conflicts of feminists and non-feminists in the movement. Part II includes both a theoretical analysis of battering and an examination of issues currently facing feminists involved in the battered women's movement: co-optation by funding agencies, the provision of services versus societal change, heterosexism and homophobia, racism, funding cutbacks, and right-wing attacks.

Wilson, Carolyn F. *Violence Against Women: An Annotated Bibliography.* Boston: G. K. Hall, 1981.

A comprehensive, book length bibliography dealing with rape, sexual abuse of children, and pornography, as well as battered women. It includes both scholarly and popular literature published, for the most part, between 1975 and August 1980, and descriptions of five other bibliographies. Useful features of this bibliography are its frequent inclusion of issues of special interest to feminists, its attempt to identify the theoretical perspective of the authors, and its attention to methodological issues.

Subject Area:
Sexual Assault

Recommendations of Judith Osborne

Boyle, Christine. "Section 142 of the Criminal Code: A Trojan Horse?" 23 *Criminal Law Quarterly* 253 (1981).

Assesses the impact of the Supreme Court's decision in *Forsythe* on s.142, as amended. It is concluded that the provision now offers minimal concrete legal protection for the rape victim who must continue to rely on the judge for protection.

Brooks, Neil. "Rape & the Laws of Evidence," 23 *Chitty's Law Journal* 1 (1975).

Discusses Canadian law concerning proof of rape; seen as a caricature of society's attitudes towards women. Focuses on the role of the victim's character and the need for corroboration and reviews actual and proposed changes to these areas.

Chappell, Duncan. "The Impact of Rape Reform Legislation: Some Comparative Trends," Paper presented at annual meeting of A.S.C., Toronto, November, 1982.

Compares process and impact of rape reform in a number of common law jurisdictions. It would appear that significant gains have been made in victim treatment. The most important change, however, has been symbolic rather than substantive.

Chappell, D., and P. Sallman. "Rape in Marriage Legislation in South Australia. Anatomy of a Reform," 14 *Australian Journal of Forensic Science* 51 (1982).

Examines amendment of marital exemption provision in South

Australian rape law: why and how it was changed and its impact.

Clark, Lorenne and Debra Lewis. *Rape: The Price of Coercive Sexuality.* Toronto: Women's Press, 1977.

> Examines rape in Canada from a general feminist perspective, using a sample of actual instances of rape to show how society and the criminal justice system respond to the rapist and the victim. Advocates the redefinition of rape as an assault with physical coercion rather than absence of consent being its central feature. Recommendations are made concerning police and courtroom practices along with a rationalization of penalties for rape.

Kasinsky, R. G. "The Rise & Institutionalization of the Anti-Rape Movement in Canada" in *Violence in Canada* ed. Gamman M.A.B. Toronto: Methuen, 1978, pp. 151-161.

> Explores the rise of the anti-rape movement, which is seen as a by-product of the feminist movement. In particular, there is a focus on the role of rape crisis centres which are portrayed as the only viable immediate alternative to a conservative criminal justice system.

Law Reform Commission of Canada. *Report No. 10: Sexual Offenses* (Ottawa: Supply & Services, 1978).

> An examination of Canadian rape law which recommends a graded scheme of sexual assault, based on the seriousness of the conduct. Also recommended are the removal of spousal immunity, the inclusion of all interpersonal sexual interference, regardless of gender or age.

Loh, Wallace, D. "Q: What has Reform of Rape Legislation Wrought? A: Truth in Criminal Labelling," *Journal of Social Issues* 37 (1981): 58

> A comparison of the impact of common law and legislation on the processing of over 400 rape cases through the criminal justice system. The number of convictions, pleas and the rate of charging remained unchanged but penalties became more certain, although not more severe as a result of a reform of the penalty structure.

McTeer, M. "Rape & the Canadian Legal Process," in *Violence in*

Canada, ed. Gammon M.A.B. Toronto: Methuen, 1978; pp. 135-150.

> An analysis of Canadian law, the options it provides and its deficiencies. Observes that legal change and attitudinal change may not coincide, and, in the absence of the latter, legal change is largely ineffective.

Pickard, Toni. "Culpable Mistakes in Rape," 30 *University of Toronto Law Journal* 75, 415 (1980).

> Proposes that mistake as to consent must be reasonable in order to exculpate. Moving beyond the subjective/objective controversy in relation to mens rea, it is recommended that mens rea should be considered within the context of the criminal conduct. The *Pappajohn* decision is evaluated in light of this position and is found to be lacking.

Sallman, P. A., and D. Chappell. *Rape Law Reform in South Australia.* Adelaide Law Review Research Paper No. 3, 1982.

> Records observations and findings of a study of major changes in South Australian rape law and allied sexual crimes. Found that attitudes toward rape becoming more enlightened.

Recommendations of Susan Caringella-MacDonald

Brownmiller, Susan. *Against Our Will: Men, Women and Rape.* New York: Simon & Schuster, 1975.

> This work remains a classic in the field. Brownmiller traces sexist attitudes and treatment of rape through history. Her feminist argument is fastidiously substantiated through in-depth analysis of rape in different circumstances such as war and riot and in everyday life. *Against Our Will* demands the rethinking of not only rape, but additionally of the power of super/subordination involved in all male-female relationships.

Chappell, D., R. Geis, and G. Geis, eds. *Forcible Rape: The Crime, the Victim, and the Offender.* New York: Columbia University Press, 1977.

> Sixteen articles, along with an introductory chapter and "Selective Bibliography," are pulled together in this volume on rape. A number of articles provide empirically based descrip-

tive profiles of victim, defendant, and case characteristics associated with this crime. Included also are significant works elaborating the discrimination and justification involved in the beliefs about and handling of forcible rape.

Field, H. S., and L. B. Bienen. *Jurors and Rape: A Study in Psychology and Law.* Lexington, Massachusetts: Lexington Books, 1980.

Part I of this book reports the findings of a study which examined the decision-making of citizens, police officers, rape crisis counselors, and rapists in rape cases. Selected demographic and attitudinal variables were analyzed as they related to decisions rendered in hypothetical rape case situations by these various groups of "potential jurors." The second part of this book begins with a superb overview of legislative change in rape statutes in the past decade. The summary of rape statutes and alteration on a state-by-state basis is a unique resource for those interested in rape law in this country.

National Institute of Law Enforcement and Criminal Justice. *Forcible Rape: Final Project Report.* Washington, D.C.: U.S. Government Printing Office, 1978.

One of the eleven research products, the *Final Project Report* summarizes the national two-year study of rape victims, offenders, and criminal justice response. Demographic data on rape are presented in the first two chapters, with the remaining five devoted to police and prosecutor training and response types and needs.

Schwendinger, Julia R. and Herman Schwendinger. *Rape and Inequality.* Beverly Hills, California: Sage Publications, 1983.

The Schwendingers are explicit and systematic in their explanation of rape in this significant new book. They begin by attempting to dispell myths, and continue to insightfully critique previous works and theories about rape. The subsequent sections draw on the work of Marx, anthropological research, and current statistical data to document the thesis that political-economy and sexual inequality are integrally tied to the violent crime of rape. The type of macroscopic theoretical approach facilitates new insights into not only the existence of rape, but also into necessary social change directed at its reduction.

Subject Area:
Prostitution

Recommendations of Marlene Beckman

Barnes, Claude T. *The White Slave Traffic Act.* Salt Lake City: Sugar House Press, 1946.

> This book by a former Supreme Court Justice traces the history and provides an analysis of the inclusion of the term "any other immoral purpose" in the White Slave Traffic Act.

Bullough, Vern and Bonnie. *Prostitution: An Illustrated Social History.* New York: Crown Publishers, Inc., 1978.

> This book is a comprehensive overview which traces prostitution from its earliest origins until modern times. The authors traveled extensively throughout most of the world conducting investigations and gathering evidence for their research.

Feldman, Egal. "Prostitution, the Alien Woman and the Progressive Imagination, 1910-1915." *American Quarterly,* 1967.

> This article provides an excellent account of the social forces which gave rise to the anti-white slavery movement and which provided the Progressive Era reformers with evidence to support their zealous attempts to eradicate commercial prostitution.

Seagle, William. "Twilight of the Mann Act." 55 *American Bar Association Journal,* 1969.

> The author traces the history of the enforcement of the Mann Act and offers evidence to support his theory that the public conception of this law has been more myth than reality. The author maintains that this law was passed in response to an authentic social evil, and its enforcement has remained consistent with the framer's original purposes. Seagle seeks to show that the Mann Act has not been used as the tool of sexual oppression which it is reputed to be.

Recommendations of Frances Bernat

Abramson, Ellicott M. "A Note on Prostitution: Victims Without

Crime—Or There's No Crime but the Victim Is Ideology." 17 *Duquesne Law Review* (1978-79), 355.

> The author discusses and criticizes several theories which advocate the decriminalization of prostitution. It is argued that the criminal law should aim to rehabilitate prostitutes in order to change their self-images and life styles.

Comments. "Anti-Prostitution Laws: New Conflicts in the Fight Against the World's Oldest Profession." 43 *Albany Law Review* (1979), 360.

> The author discusses constitutional problems which arise in regard to prostitution laws designed to proscribe loitering or solicitation conduct. Recommendations which seek to balance state interests with individuals' rights are proposed. Such recommendations include: requiring "reasonable inquiry" before an arrest may be made; describing the particular conduct to be proscribed; and fully expounding the terms of the offense.

Comments. "Decriminalization of Prostitution: The Limits of the Criminal Law." 55 *Oregon Law Review* (1976), 553.

> The author analyzes and rejects the most common reasons given for proscription of prostitution and argues for its decriminalization. The author states that legalization of prostitution is not a viable alternative to the problems raised by prostitution proscription because legalization would require the state to spend huge amounts of money on regulating prostitution and the collection of the prostitutes' fees.

Jennings, M. Anne. "The Victim as Criminal: A Consideration of California's Prostitution Law." 64 *California Law Review* (1976), 1235.

> The article begins by discussing the nature of prostitution, rationales for its criminalization, and the realities of prostitution law enforcement. The author argues that "discreet prostitution" should be legalized, while overt public solicitation should be proscribed. Additionally, it is argued that legislative reform of prostitution laws should seek increased enforcement against pimps and provide alternatives for those wishing to leave "the life." Judicial remedies to protect individuals (women) from villation of their right of privacy and selective enforcement of the law are also discussed.

Notes. "Right of Privacy Challenges to Prostitution Statues." 58 *Washington University Law Quarterly* (1980), 439.

> The author analyzes whether prostitution's commercial nature affects an individual's right of privacy which exists in a private (non-commercial) setting. An analysis of the right of privacy is presented. The author concludes that there should be a difference between proscription of commercial sex (acts of prostitution occurring in a private setting) and solicitation for commercial sex (acts occurring in a public setting). However, the author is pessimistic about the success of such challenges in the future.

Parnas, Raymond I. "Legislative Reform of Prostitution Laws: Keeping Commercial Sex Out of Sight and Out of Mind." 21 *Santa Clara Law Review* (1981), 669.

> The purpose of this article is to help state legislatures reform their prostitution laws. The author proposes a balanced approach: proscribe public prostitution, but not private prostitution; proscribe public prostitution and patronizing equally; and, punish pimps more severely.

Richards, David A. J. "Commercial Sex and the Rights of the Person: A Moral Argument for the Decriminalization of Prostitution." 127 *University of Pennsylvania Law Review* (1979), 1195.

> This article reviews the history of prostitution and arguments for its criminalization. The author argues for decriminalization of prostitution on moral grounds and indicates that weak arguments exists for its proscription. In this regard, the author indicates that prostitution is "one of the colorful amenities of life" and should be accepted as an "inextricable part of urban life." Punishment for prostitution by the state, then, violates an individual's right to sexual autonomy and unduly restricts its availability.

Rosenbleet, Charles, and Pariente, Barbara J. "The Prostitution of the Criminal Law." 11 *American Criminal Law Review* (1973), 373.

> The purpose of this article is to discuss constitutional issues raised by prostitution laws. The authors aim their inquiry at the judiciary since legislative reform did not appear to be forthcoming. Equal protection and right of privacy arguments ap-

pear to the authors to be the most viable method to attack prostitution proscription.

Shouvlin, David P: "Preventing the Sexual Exploitation of Children: A Model Act." 17 *Wake Forest Law Review,* 535.

The article discusses 3 forms of sexual exploitation of children, including child prostitution. An act is proposed which, in regard to child prostitution, would proscribe pimping and patronizing activity as serious offenses. Child prostitutes, under the proposed code, would not be fined, but, instead placed in a treatment facility designed to rehabilitate them.

HV 6250.4 .W65 C75 1985

Criminal justice, politics, and women

DATE DUE

MAY 16 2000

Demco, Inc. 38-293